A TASTE OF PASTE

Poems for the Classroom

Written by
Thena Smith

Edited by
Linda LaTourelle
and
CC Milam

www.theultimateword.com
270 · 251 · 3600

Taste of Paste: Poems for the Classroom—copyright © 2005 by Thena Smith. ALL RIGHTS RESERVED. Permission is hereby granted, with purchase, to reproduce any part of this book on a limited basis for "personal use only."

No part of this book may be reproduced or transmitted in any form by any means, electronic or mechanical, including photocopying and recording, or by any information storage and retrieval system, without the prior permission of the publisher. Commercial use of any/all of this book requires written permission and any licensing fees, if applicable, from Bluegrass Publishing, Inc.

For information write:
Bluegrass Publishing, Inc.
PO Box 634
Mayfield, KY 42066 USA
service@theultimateword.com
www.BluegrassPublishing.com

ISBN: 0-9761925-2-7

1st Edition
Mayfield, KY : Bluegrass Publishing, Inc. 2005

Cover Design: Todd Jones, Tennessee
Proudly printed in the United States of America

Table of Contents

	Table of Contents		134	Lessons to Learn
	Dedication		147	My Hero
	Taste of Paste		150	Sports & Sportsmanship
9	Dear Teacher		160	Time For Fun
11	My Love For		164	Animal Soup
13	Teachers & Teaching		169	Scouting
44	Sunday School Teachers		176	Miscellaneous Poems
47	From A Teacher		181	When I Grow Up
49	School Staff		186	Difficult Situations
57	With Gratitude		188	Birthdays
58	The Big Yellow Bus		193	Holidaze
60	Retirement		201	Hugs
68	Early School Days		203	Attitudes
82	Grade by Grade		205	Fun to Read Aloud
93	Rules & Report Cards		219	Thank You From Thena
99	Summer Vacation		220	About the Author
100	Back to School		221	Our Favorite Sites
102	Classroom Traditions		222	Info About Our Books
109	Teen Life		223	New Books
114	Kids R Sick		224	The End
119	Seasons & Weather		225	Your Favorite Poems
125	Special Kids		227	Order Form

Dedication

First, I want to dedicate this book to my Creator with all love, honor and thanksgiving. Secondly, I dedicate this book with thanks to my wonderful and much loved husband, Ron and daughter, Melissa, for the joy they bring to my life daily.

And I must not forget my brother, Gale Cullen (see Gale, you are right at the first of the book) and Donald Cullen, who inspired me from my early days by singing little ditties to me and keeping me on my toes!

Gale, I also include your wonderful team at Farmington Elementary School. They are such a blessing to you and an inspiration to me.

Also, I must include my thanks to Terry and Ed Johnson, Andrea Cullen, Sandra Cullen, and Jill and Greg Cullen, and my lovely nieces, Marcy, Janet, Laura and Kelly.

Also, a shout out to my cousin, Marilyn King who used to sit on the steps with me and write poems, one after the other for hours.

I do not want to forget all my friends throughout the years who have inspired, strengthened, and encouraged me: Lanell Sanders, Shirley Stoeckel and Sharon Hammond and Sandra Wolfe. Thank you to each one of you!

P.S. If you have read this far and your name is not here, the dedication will be continued in my next book!

Hugs,

Trena Smith

Taste of Paste

Oh, I love to go to school
And I love to use the paste.
I love to use it for my crafts
But I really love the taste!

I know I really shouldn't say it,
But I think that it's a waste,
To hold two pages together
With something as yummy as paste!

When the bell rings to call us for lunch,
I watch the kids that brought a bunch,
But nothing in their lunch bags taste
As good as my delicious paste!

Teacher sent a note to Mom
And in the note I read
That I could no longer bring my paste,
I must use glue instead!

I think it's really sad
And I hope it won't catch on
For what will I do, when all I have is glue
And all the yummy paste is gone??

I like a teacher who gives you something to take home to think about besides homework.

–Lily Tomlin
as "Edith Ann"

Dear Teacher...

I have a soft spot in my heart for teachers! I was one briefly and my daughter is now a teacher, too! My whole family values education and enjoys the thrill of learning.

After "Where's Thena? I need a poem about..." was published, I had numerous requests from teachers asking for something just for them-well, ok, at least five! I put aside the work I was compiling and jumped right into something that I hope not only scrapbookers, moms and crafters can use, but that public and private school teachers, as well as, home school teachers will be able to use in their homes and classroom.

Teachers are such an important part of our country. They are the underpaid and sometimes underappreciated unsung heroes of our community. I wanted to do something to show them how special they are and to provide you with a few verses to show your appreciation for teachers, as well as, to provide teachers with a way to express their appreciation for the rest of the staff, the parents, and the children in their care.

Not every poem in this book is exclusively for teachers and not all specifically mention teachers, teaching or school, but a number of them do. Included are poems that speak of every day topics that come up in homes and classrooms, geared from the youngest child up to teens.

There are poems to give to teachers and staff for appreciation, retirement, birthdays or just thinking of you cards. There are subjects pertaining to mommies sending kids off for the first day, teachers welcoming kids into their classrooms, and even, the view point of the students having to go to school.

Also, included are poems about holidays, sports, special needs, photo days and other miscellaneous topics that might be discussed or studied by the class or just as poems to read to the class and share as they have a quiet time.

Please freely use these poems to share and bless others. In some cases, people only need a short verse to complete the task they have at hand. I do not mind at all if you need to take a small portion to use. Please list my name as author so that these little verses and poems do not become the works of that "anonymous" writer that pops up everywhere!

It is my sincere prayer you find something in this book to cheer you, inspire you, enlighten you and brighten your day. May you share these inspirations with others and touch their hearts. When you are blessed and others are blessed by the thoughts in this book, then my goal for this book will have been met!

Hugs,

Trena Smith

Poems for the Classroom

My Love for Teachers

When I started first grade. I was pretty shy around teachers. I had a lovely teacher for first grade and her husband was the principal. She was all business and very efficient and he was more fun loving. He called my brothers and me. Big Cullen. Cullen. and Little Cullen. if we got into trouble or rated his attention. I was "Little Cullen."

I was once the reason for extreme embarrassment for my brothers. We had missed the bus and then. encountered car trouble and were late to school. The rule was that you spent noon recess in the office if you were tardy. Well. there we were. the whole Cullen tribe and the principal asked first grader. Little Cullen. to read for him. Oh. I can still remember the selection I proudly read "Ting-a-ling. Ting-a-ling went the bell on the gate." I could not understand why my older brothers were not bursting with pride.

In second grade. I was inspired by my teacher. She was the reason that I decided I to be a teacher when I grew up. She was very kind and mellow and grandmotherly. She seemed so old to me at the time. but when I went back and taught briefly in that same school. she was still there along with another favorite. my third grade teacher.

My school years were lovely and I enjoyed it until seventh grade. when we moved to town. I was not only the new girl in school. but the tall. skinny. freckled new girl! I did have

continued...

11

Taste of Paste

...continued from previous page

some teachers that encouraged me and recognized in me some qualities and values that I didn't even see in myself. I am so thankful for such teachers!

When I started my career, I taught fifth grade, which appropriately enough, was the only grade in which I mildly acted up when in grade school—I talked a lot! I taught only briefly because hubby was called into the Navy to active duty before I finished my last year of college. At that time, I was teaching on an emergency certificate. I loved every minute of my teaching career. The kids cried at Christmas time when I left to go be with my hubby.

Because of the wonderful experience in teaching children, I have a soft spot in my heart for teachers. (And the fact that my daughter is a teacher.) I also have a special love and affection for the underdog, the skinny kid, the kid with freckles and the kid chosen last. You will find some of these feelings reflected occasionally throughout my poetry.

I am pleased to share these words in poetic form for you to use in your scrapbooking and journaling. You may also find enjoyment in simply reading for fun and relaxation. My hope is that these poems might bless you or someone you know.

I want to be a teacher.
I want to train a child.
I want to give hope and confidence
That's what makes me smile!

Poems for the Classroom

Teachers & Teaching

A Teacher is Someone

A teacher is someone who looks you in the eyes
When you accomplish your dream or goal
And just says, "I'm not at all surprised!"

A teacher is someone who takes you by your hand
When there are things you just don't understand,
And holds on until you catch up once more
Then smiles and says, "That's what a teacher is for!"

A teacher is someone who no matter what or where
Is always ready and willing to share.
We look in your eyes and know that it is true
For we see that kind of teacher in you.

Dear Teacher

I'm sending you my child today
To train and teach and such.
She is a special child
And I love her very much.

I know it may seem strange
For a mom to write to you,
But when a young one starts to school
What is a loving mom to do?

I want her to be respectful
And learn her lessons too;
That's why I am so very thankful
For the good example that is you.

13

Taste of Paste

Thank You

You have been such a wonderful blessing
And such a lovely friend.
You have taken such lovely care of our children
And your patience has no end.

You have cuddled and nurtured.
You have taught and played games.
You have instructed and consoled.
And kissed away hurts on tiny frames.

There is no way to truly show you
Just how special you are today.
But we will try to give you just a hint
By sending our heartfelt thanks your way.

Recipe for A Great Teacher

Take one big cup of compassion
And mix in bits of fun
With the ability to see bright skies
Even when there is no sun.

Add several dashes of hope
And bits of creativity
And the love of being
Busy as a bee.

Stir this all together
(And this is the most important part)
Pour the mixture inside
One gigantic and loving heart!

Poems for the Classroom

It's a New School Year

It's a brand new year
And a brand new day
With lots of new adventures
Coming your way.

We are here to help you
And guide you,
To take you by the hand,
So that all of the new things
You will understand.

The thoughts of brand new subjects
May sound a bit scary to you now,
But you will learn how to handle them expertly
For we will show you how.

Teachers know the feelings
That you face at the brand new year.
The excitement and anticipation
Mixed with a bit of fear.

So each one of us is committed
To helping teach our brand new class,
How to master all things now foreign,
So that with flying colors you will pass!

Teachers
Guide With Love

How Teachers are Made

I sent my daughter off to school
And from days so early on.
"I want to be a teacher"
Was her little song.

She played with dollies
As she read them her picture books
And when I glanced into her room
It had a certain familiar look.

Her chairs were lined up in rows
And at each one sat a doll
With picture book and paper
And crayons with which to draw.

Years later she went to college
And education was her degree.
But in my heart I knew
How this teacher came to be.

For I believe that teachers
Have a very special heart.
And for this awesome calling
God has chosen them from the start.

"I want to be a teacher" Was her little song...

Poems for the Classroom

To Teach

To teach children is my dream.
I want to instruct and train.
I want to tutor others.
And add information to the brain.

I want to instill values in little ones
To enlighten them and inform.
I want to help ground them
And fit them for the purpose
For which they were born.

I want to coach my team of students.
I want to drill them in their lessons.
I want to give them instruction.
And help answer all their questions.

I want to be there for them
And guide them as they study.
I want to be their mentor
And not just another buddy.

Lord, help me to be these things
And other things that children need.
And with your help and guidance
I know I can succeed.

I'm doing my bit
to make America great!
I'm teaching the children!

Taste of Paste

Thank You, Ms. Janet

This is a little poem to say
Thank you for the loving way
You take care of our little ones-
Our little daughters and little sons.

You focus on each tiny frame
And know the needs that fit each name.
As valuable to a child as the teaching you do
Is receiving a big hug from you.

You do special things each day
To help each child in work or play.
Your attention to important issues from the start
Endear you to each mommy's heart.

So, thank you Ms. Janet for the way
You perform your job each day.
I know that it's more than just a job to you
For your loving nature comes shining through.

Teachers Share

Teachers share their world with you
They share what they hold in their heart
They want each child to enjoy the world
And embrace life from the start.

My Success is Their Success!

Poems for the Classroom

Teacher Survival Kit

As you start a brand new school year,
I put together some helpful gear.
First to make your mistakes disappear,
Please find an eraser here.
And just so you will always have money,
This penny—though it may seem funny!
And socks to wear upon your feet,
If the winters are cold and you can't afford heat!
And many times we hear it said,
That we lose all the marbles in our head.
make sure that never comes true,
A gift of marbles just for you.
Rubber bands to help you stretch and not break,
Some aspirin, just in case,
Pain relievers you need to take.
And hugs and kisses in this bag,
In case your blood sugar starts to lag.

T eachers
E ducate
A ll
C hildren's
H earts and minds
E nduring long hours
R eadily
S acrificing their own time.

Taste of Paste

Teaching A B C's

A is for a positive attitude
that a teacher must have each day

B is for the books
from which a teacher earns her pay

C is for children
teaching them is her career

D is for the discipline
that sometimes children fear

E is for the effort
expended every day in serious things

F is fun things such as field trips
that sometimes come her way

G is for the grades
in such things as geography

H is for holidays
from school that make the kids so happy

I is for instruction
with imagination and flair

Poems for the Classroom

J is for the job
she does in being just and fair

K is for knowledge
which offers the keys to success

L is for learning life's lessons
and teaching them with finesse

M is for the millions of meetings
she must attend each year

N means it's the nature of the job
with extra duties sometimes unclear

O is for order
that must be kept in the class

P is for parents
whose test you must pass

Q is for quizzes with questions
not too difficult for the class

R is for report cards
to tell them "You Pass"

S is for skills
and lessons to be taught

Taste of Paste

T is for tests to see
if they learned as they ought

U is for understanding
and being unique

V is for so valuable
are the words that you speak

W is for wisdom
that comes from above

Making you "X"-tra special
teaching the kids that we love

Y is for You are
such a wonderful gift

Z is for your zest for teaching
that gives us such a lift

So here you have it.
A through Z.
Telling you just how grateful
We are to have teachers like you!

ABC & 123
Thanks So Much
For Teaching Me!

Poems for the Classroom

I Need a Teacher

I need a teacher with a kind heart.
A teacher who isn't afraid to care
About the lives of her students-
A teacher who loves to share.

I need to see a smile on her face
And to feel comfortable
In speaking to her each day.
One who listens to what students say.

I need to see in a teacher's eyes
That she really does care for me.
And all of the others in her class-
It should be easy to see.

I need a teacher who laughs with me
And who understands the need for fun-
A teacher whose smiling face
Signals the day has begun.

To find that teacher
Was such sheer delight
And if you surmise
I'm speaking of you-
Well. you are absolutely right!

If I can reach them,
I can teach them!

Taste of Paste

God Bless the Teacher

And as I send my child to school each day
There is a little prayer I say:
"Lord, I ask that the teachers be kind
To this precious child of mine."

When there are duties that parents share
And I have reason to visit there
I have another little prayer:
"Lord, bless the teacher!"

"Oh, Lord," I've prayed as I watch you,
"Give her the strength for all she must do
And give her wisdom straight from you...
Oh, Lord, bless the teacher!"

I see how hard you work each day
To help children learn to work and play.
I see your tender loving way...
And even more I stop and say:
"Lord, help the teacher!"

When your day is really tough
And you feel you've had enough,
Just remember that there are those who care
And remember you in daily prayer...
"Lord, Bless You Teacher!"

A Teacher Is One Boss Who Wants Everyone To Succeed!

Poems for the Classroom

Homeschool Teacher

Homeschooling can be such a blessing
Bonding with your child in such a way
That it gives them new respect
For what their mom, as teacher, might say.

It involves hope in the future
And learning from the past
With the desire to instill in your child
Wisdom and knowledge that will last.

There is so much that must work together-
Each item is an integral part
Of all that makes a great homeschool teacher
Most important being a mom's willing heart!

I'm Taught at Home

I'm taught at home,
And don't have to leave each day,
To learn about the world around me
Or to be in a classroom play!

I love the fun of being home,
And learning with my mother,
For I have a teacher
Who cares for me like no other.

Maybe when I am older,
I may want to venture out,
But I'm learning every day
And that's what school's about!

Taste of Paste

A Teacher Watches

A good teacher watches
As students come and go
And she remembers special things
That each individual brings.

There are those who are the smart kids
The ones who never have to study
And the ones who love to socialize
And be everybody's buddy.

There are those who are so shy
And fear that they don't fit in
And those who seem uncomfortable
In their very own skin.

I watch and wait for time to show me
The things that I can do
To make their lives easier
The whole school year through.

And to the student it may seem chance
That led me to them that day
And may think it was by accident
The words they heard me say.

But a good teacher listens every day
And tries to meet each need
And give each special student
The encouragement needed to succeed!

Poems for the Classroom

Prayer from a Teacher

"Lord, please give me compassion,
In a heart that loves a bit of fun.
Let me always see sunny skies-
Look through the clouds and see the sun!

Fill me with hope, Father,
And please grant me creativity
Along with the love of being always
The best teacher I can be.

Lord, please make my heart big enough
For this all to fit inside.
And, Father, grant me loving arms
That are always open wide."

Parents as Teachers

Parents know the words
To the songs their children sing.
They are the best teachers
The ones who can give their children wings.

Homeschool teachers are fine examples
Of being willing to share
Their lives, their day, their very heart
With children entrusted to their care.

Teachers make writing exciting and learning inviting!

Taste of Paste

Mean Ole Teacher

I had a mean ole teacher
Ms. Mary was her name.
And she was awful to me
Every day I came!

She made me sit down in my seat
When the bell would ring.
And looked for mistakes I made-
I mean every little thing!!

She made me late for recess
By making me get in line.
And she always knew on sight
Which spitball might be mine!

She made me go to lunch
When I wanted to play ball-
But wait until I tell you
The meanest thing of all!

She made me come to school each day
And told me if I was late.
I'd get sent to the principal's office
And have to sit in a chair and wait.

So, folks would come and go past me
And know just why I was there.
And they would point their fingers-
Oh, life just isn't very fair!

—continued

Poems for the Classroom

-continued from previous page

She said that telling lies
Was not the right thing to do
And somehow if I tried one-
Ms. Mary always knew!

Ohhhhhh. she was a meanie!
She was one of a kind
And because she was such a meanie.
I hope she teaches each kid of mine!!!

Thanks For Your Trust

Thank you parents for trusting me
With your most valuable treasures.
I know that the worth of each little one
Is something beyond all measure.

I do not take it lightly
That you entrust them to my care.
And give you my word of honor
That your love for them I share.

I understand the concern you have
That your child be treated well each day.
And your desire for their health and safety
Whether at their work or at their play.

Your child is safe here in my care
And I treasure their moments here.
For I chose to be a guardian of these tiny souls
When I chose teaching as my career.

Taste of Paste

God Created Teachers

God created some special folks
And in the world he gave each one a part.
For those He would use as teachers
He gave a special kind of heart.

He gave them a heart that would listen
To what a child would say,
One that would respond to what they heard
In a very loving way.

He created a heart that would long to nurture
And would not be easily pained.
But even if it was wounded
Would not hesitate to be involved again.

He placed this heart in hand chosen ones
Instilling in them the desire to teach.
And with the special God given heart
Millions of children these teachers reach.

Our Ms. Pat was one in a million
For she got a double dose
Her heart reaches out to all she sees
And that's why we love her the most!

We hope she will not leave us
And that she will consent to stay
For our hearts are joined with hers now
In a wonderful and special way!

Poems for the Classroom

Eighteen Students

Eighteen classmates
Starting the year together
Coming to share your day
In fair or stormy weather.

No snow could prevent you
From doing the best you could
And even your snow day
You turned into something good.

You colored pages for this book
And smiled when asked to pose
And as for frowns or such
We saw none of those.

This is just a little note
To say that we have been blessed
To have such wonderful kids as you
For you are certainly the best!

Teacher

Courage is a teacher.
Wisdom is one. too.
Love is the teacher's heart
Where she with love
Combines the other two.

A teacher puts the "fun" in fundamental!

Taste of Paste

Kids Need a Teacher

Kids need a teacher who likes to teach
And likes each student in her care.
A teacher who loves to instruct-
A teacher who loves to share.

Kids need to see a friendly face
And feel a gentle spirit.
They need to know that when they speak
Their teacher is going to hear it.

They need to see in a teacher's eyes
The love that she has for each one.
And all of the others in her class
Every parent's daughter or son!

Kids need a teacher who laughs with ease
And who understands the need for fun.
A teacher whose smiling face
Signals the day has begun.

Some search for this kind of teacher
Until their school years are through.
But our kids were very fortunate
To find that teacher in you!

Kids need a teacher who likes to teach!

Poems for the Classroom

Why Should I Be a Teacher?

"Why should I be a teacher?"
I heard myself say.
I could do something else
And leave my cares at the end of the day.

Why should I be a teacher,
When though I must be highly educated?
I am usually the professional underpaid
And sometimes underappreciated.

Why should I become a teacher
And spend my career in school
Teaching not only the three R's
But trying to instill the Golden Rule?

Why should I face the queries
That sometimes come my way
About why some teachers get the summer off
And have bankers hours each day?

Why should I want to teach
And constantly be under government scrutiny
And sometimes face a classroom
Where kids seem to want to mutiny?

The reason is simple
That it amazes me...
I must be a teacher
For that's what I was meant to be!

I must be a teacher...
I was meant to be!

Taste of Paste

No Teacher Left Behind

They set the rules and guidelines
And the President says, "Fine.
We are all for education—
No child left behind!"

The classroom faces struggles.
The teachers all work so hard.
They want to pass each student,
But their bodies are so tired.

They fight a mighty battle.
They do the best they can,
To do the things they need to do,
And meet the state's demands.

But I think we should reconsider,
And that it should now be time
To treat our teachers with respect
And leave not one behind!!

Who Decides?

Who decides to be a teacher
And just how does one decide?
Do they always know that they must teach
From the feelings they have inside?

Other jobs are more prestigious
And pay more than a teacher's salary,
But none can offer the reward you seek
If a teacher you are destined to be!

Poems for the Classroom

Ten Reasons Why Teaching is the Best Job in the World

1. You are needed by the community, the nation and the children.

2. You have the opportunity to see the excitement on a child's face as they learn new things.

3. You find rewards in unexpected places, the light of recognition in a child's eyes, a handmade Valentine or a shy hug as a child runs out the door.

4. You never know when you may be teaching a future astronaut, president or famous artist.

5. You touch lives each day and make not only a lasting impression, but an eternal one.

6. You are in a position to teach, help, inspire, encourage and enlighten. So, you may be remembered in years to come as the person who most inspired a child to be the wonderful person they became.

7. You will be recognized by most of the community and never have to attend any function as a stranger.

8. You will be quoted often (and misquoted!)

9. You will learn something new every day and be blessed!

10. And most importantly–any ten to twenty-five students in your classroom!

Back to School!

Your holiday is over now
And back to school you go.
I know that it is difficult
For you have told me so!

And even though you might think
That it would be rather cool.
You cannot play hooky
You must go back to school!

I understand your problem
That it can be a pain
And you have gotten accustomed
To freedom once again!

But listen to me carefully.
I hate to sound like a preacher
But you must go back to school
Because. well. you're the TEACHER!!

Attention Dear Teachers

You must go to school
I know it is difficult
But that is the rule!

A Good Teacher is A Precious Gift

Poems for the Classroom

Thank You Teacher

You have done so very much
To help each child this year
Encouraging them to reach for the stars
And of failure to hold no fear.

You inspired them to do their best
As they came to school each day.
Ms. Marcia, it is with heartfelt appreciation
That we send our thanks your way.

We created this little album
To show you how much we care
In its pages are many memories
For you to enjoy and to share.

You Are...

You are a wonderful teacher
Who gives each heart a lift
By the wonderful way
You go about your day
And you are a wonderful gift!

You are a gift to each student
And they love you so much
For there is a special quality in you
That allows you each heart to touch.

Great Teacher's Inspire
By Lighting A Fire

Taste of Paste

When the Garden is a Child

I looked into my garden
And saw there in neat rows,
All sorts of beauty from nature
The planted things I chose.

I looked at the rich soil
That was evident around it,
And realized how important
Are the plants which will surround it.

Our children are like this garden
With a mind that is pure and fresh,
Ready to be cultivated,
Nourished and enriched.

The teacher who can break up the soil
And prepare it for the child to learn,
Will foster the growth of this little mind
And rewards of great affection will earn.

A teacher with a heart that listens
To what each child will say,
Further encourages the seeds of knowledge
That she has sent their way.

She tends this garden through the year
And does the best she can do,
But she can only do so much
The rest is up to you.

continued...

Poems for the Classroom

...continued from previous page

Surround this fertile little garden
This precious and inquisitive mind,
With love and nourishment every day
So that there will be flowers on each vine.

Each bud will turn into a bloom;
Each vine will bear its fruit;
Each little blossom will be a lovely flower,
And this little shrub will have a strong, deep root.

This is life's most precious garden—
Tend it with devotion and love.
For this very special little garden
Is treasured and blessed by God above.

Just Look at Them

Look at them sitting there,
Each one tall and straight in their chair!
How special is each to me
Do you think that they can see
That I have no teacher's pet—
All are special to me and yet...
There is something unique in
Every single one
Oh what joy, life holds
For those so young!

T is for Teacher, Tenderhearted, Touching, Testing!

Taste of Paste

Teachers Pet

As a teacher.
I never forget
That I can't
Have a teacher's "pet."

But in a classroom
Of 28 or 29.
It may be hard to find a way
For each child to shine.

So each week
We choose a child of the week.
And focus on the qualities
That make them unique!

I'm Teacher's Pet

Look at me!
I'm the teacher's pet.
I don't want you
To ever forget!

It doesn't matter
What you think anyway;
I know that it's true
So that's what I say.

I'm not really this confident
As a general rule.
But I know I'm the pet
'Cause my mom home schools!

My Kids

Johnny looked on Randy's paper
When he didn't see me look
And hid his cheat sheet
Behind his big notebook.
Randy saw me looking
But didn't want me to know
That he saw Johnny peeking
And he won't tell me so.
Susan was almost in tears
When she saw we had a test
And I know at lunchtime
I will have all of them at my desk!

Remind Me

"Remind me, Lord, why do I teach?"
I asked God one day.
And then I looked outside
To see the little ones at play.

They were sitting on the playground
Each one in a line.
With Suzie as the teacher
And the name she used was mine!

They were playing school,
Which was wonderful to see.
But Suzie was playing teacher
And she was playing ME!

Taste of Paste

What Do You Give a Teacher

What do you give a teacher
Who does so much for you.
Not only on the holiday
But each day the whole year through?

How do you say thank you
For the gift she daily gives.
And the examples of good citizenship
By the way this teacher lives?

When do you take a moment
To do a bit of sharing.
To tell this teacher thank you
For all her warmth and caring?

Well, we hope this little card
Will give you a little hint
Of how wonderful we think you are
For with it—lots of love is sent!

Thank You

Just a little note to say
Thank you. Parents.
You've made my day!
Your thoughtfulness
And unique loving gift
Give my heart
Such a happy lift!
A teacher always loves to know
That she is helping students
To learn and to grow!

Poems for the Classroom

A Teacher

A teacher is more than an instructor
More than just a guide.
A teacher must look at each child
And see the precious worth inside!

A teacher is more than a leader
But must lead the children each day.
A teacher must listen to a child's heart
Not just to the words they say.

Sometimes we have the rare privilege
Of a teacher that is beyond compare.
And you are one of those teachers—
The answer to a parent's prayer!

Thank You Parents

Thank you parents
for making my day.
By the kind thoughts
You sent my way.

A teacher loves to know
That she is appreciated, too.
And it is so special
To receive cards from you!

If You Can Read This,
Thank A Teacher!

Taste of Paste

Sunday School Teachers

Ms. Pat, Zachary and Jesus

God created some special folks
And in the world he gave each one a part.
For those He would use as teachers
He gave a special kind of heart.

He gave them a heart that would listen
To what a child would say
And one that would respond to what they heard
In a very loving way.

Our Ms. Pat is one in a million
For she got a double dose
Her heart reaches out to all she sees
And that's why we love her the most!

She has shown our Zachary Jesus
In a very special way
Filled him up with the love of God
That forever in his heart will stay.

When we get to Heaven
I want to thank God personally
For the teachers like Ms. Pat
Who taught my little Zachary!

Thank You for Giving To the Lord By Giving to Me!

Poems for the Classroom

Find Me A Task

Lord, give me a task-
Either great or small
But something I can do for you.
I'll go where you want me to go,
Do what you want me to do.
I would go to darkest continents,
Pitch my tent there in the dirt
Until I had ministered to your people
And comforted those who hurt.
I would ride out on a camel
In the desert dry and dreary:
I would teach the world of you
Though I might be tired and weary.
I would gladly die for Jesus:
I would give my life for you.
So, find for me, dear Father,
A job that I can do!
Lord, I'll do what you would have me do
Heal the sick, the lame, and the blind
But, Lord, teaching kids in Sunday School
Is not what I had in MIND!!!

God Bless Those Who Teach

God bless those who teach
In Sunday School
Please let them have each day
Your gentle and loving guidance
As they share with those you send their way.

45

Taste of Paste

The Note

The bulletin board had a note
And I smiled as I read.
"You should be teaching Sunday School
Instead of sleeping late in bed!"

It really made me stop and think
About the things I love so much
And each of them was taught to me
By someone's gentle touch.

So I began to consider teaching
And pondered until I knew
That teaching kids about their faith
Was something I should do!

I no longer sleep in on Sunday!
I'm up and out the door.
And now I realize
I love Sundays even more!

Wake Up Sleepy Head!

Wake up sleepy head!
No time to waste-
Don't stay in bed!
Take a shower
And put on a dress.
You really want to look your best!
The kids are waiting
And so's the preacher
For their favorite
Sunday school teacher!

Poems for the Classroom

From A Teacher

Apples

They set them on my desk.
They set them on my chair.
I can hardly walk around the room
For there are apples everywhere.

It isn't that I don't like apples—
I think they're good to eat.
Especially the juicy red ones
That taste so crisp and sweet.

I have stuffed ones made of velvet.
Ceramic ones so shiny and fine.
Decanter apples, if you can imagine,
Filled with a tiny bit of wine.

I have bright red plastic ones
And wooden ones so spiffy.
You tell me the type you want,
I can find one in a jiffy.

Each one carried by tiny hands
And lovingly brought to me.
That's why I can't bear to part
With a single one, you see!

But after 20 years of teaching...
Of apples I have had my share—
So perhaps next year at Christmas
Someone will send me a
...Pear?

Taste of Paste

Little Butterflies

Like shy little caterpillars they came
On that very first day.
A bit afraid of what would happen here
And not sure of what to say.

But soon they joined in and started to grow
Filling their minds with wonderful things;
The more they learned
The more they wanted to know.

The tiny pupils were like the pupa
Holding onto the teacher for the support
As they were taught each day
Work really seemed as much fun as play!

Then suddenly one day we saw
In each pupa's place
Beautiful little butterflies
Flitting about the room with such grace!

Spreading delicate wings
And carrying pollen of love and joy
From flower to flower
Was each little girl and boy.

From the shy little caterpillars that entered these doors
Have emerged beautiful little butterflies
Happily reflecting the beauty of God's love
As they try their new wings in the sunshine.

So go little butterflies to Kindergarten
And enjoy what you have learned
For you have certainly earned
Those lovely little wings!

Poems for the Classroom

School Staff

The Principal of the Thing

Our school is the best!
It is never second rate.
Our staff is superb.
And our students are just great!

Our lawn is nicely mowed.
The parking lot is smooth.
And we keep perfect track
Of all the supplies we use.

The food at lunch is good.
And kids say it's delicious.
While the parents testify
That it seems to be nutritious.

The bells all ring on time
And the hallways are neat and clean
Because the janitors are great
And wonderful human beings.

We have a catchy school song
That all the kids can sing.
What is the secret to our success?
It's the "Principal" of the thing!!

A teacher can incite students to write!

49

Taste of Paste

The Sub

We had a substitute today
In my English class.
I knew Ms. Johnson wasn't there
Since I go to English last.
I overheard kids talking in the hall
About the things they would do
To tease the substitute teacher
Before the hour was through.
But the substitute was wise to them.
And before she came in the door.
She listened in the hallway
For five minutes, maybe more.
She nipped their plans in the bud
And now they all think she's cool.
Seems she knew what they would do
For she once went to this same school...

Poor Substitute

Pity the poor substitute
Who must take the place
Of a much loved teacher
And her students must face.
No matter what she does
She feels it is going to be wrong
Whether doing flashcards
Or leading in a song.
For the kids who love a teacher
Can see no one else at her desk
And won't relax and settle down
Except for the one they like the best!

Poems for the Classroom

Thank You Special Ed Teacher

God created some special folks
And in the world he gave each one a part.
For those He would use as teachers
He gave a special kind of heart.
He gave them a heart that would listen
To what a child would say.
One that would respond to what they heard
In a very loving way.
He placed this heart in hand-chosen ones
And instilled in them the desire to teach
And with the special God given heart
They would nurture the children within their reach.
And for those whose heart was purest
The Father would impart
A love for those special kids
So dear to our Father's heart.
These kids are the ones who need love the most
But seem so often to be left out.
The ones whose mind and spirit
Is filled with longing and self-doubt.
You are one in a million
Hand-chosen by God above
To teach, love and nurture
And shower upon them the Father's love!
How does one thank you
There are no words to say
But I know that God is looking on from Heaven
To bless you on this your special day!

Taste of Paste

Unsung Heroes

Our school has unsung heroes
That we see every day.
Some feed us in the cafeteria
Others watch us when we play.

One might be the principal.
Who is a pal to all.
One might be a teacher's aid
Or sub who answers an early morning call.

The janitor keeps our school so neat
And lets no trash or litter
Get a foothold on our campus and
Believe me. he's no quitter!

The groundskeeper keeps the grounds green and neat
Before the winter season comes
And to the cold. wind or snow
The green leaves and grass succumb.

The secretary is always there
And on the job is she.
Keeping track of everything
And just where everyone should be.

Yes. there are unsung heroes
Filling this building every day.
So let us take this opportunity
To send a bit of praise their way!

Hug A Helper!

Poems for the Classroom

Playground Supervisor

Some kids are on the monkey bars
And others on the slide.
Some are playing kickball
All glad to be outside.
Some kids hate tetherball
But jump ropes are their thing.
And as they throw the rope
They chant a bit and sing.
My job is to watch each child
With eagle eyes unblinking
And try to know what they'll do next
And know what they are thinking!
My pockets must hold Band-Aids
And my face must wear a smile.
For each day on the playground
They are my kids for a while.
I try to get them nice and quiet
Before we all go back in.
Some days I lose that battle
And other days I win.
But no matter how the day goes
When a child smiles sweetly at me
I know just why this job
Had a definite appeal for me!
Hugs and smiles are special
And I treasure them each one.
They make my day go faster
And make my job more fun.
I may not get rich or famous
But here is where I do my part.
To watch over children as they play
And add my loving touch to each child's heart.

Taste of Paste

School Playground Prayer

As a teacher I am a trusted guardian
Of each child in my care.
And with every recess
I say this little prayer.

"God bless those on the slides and swings
And protect those on the teeter-totter.
Let not a single child be hurt
Not anyone's son or daughter.

Let me be diligent in watching
As they have their playtime fun.
And I ask that you send guardian angels, Lord,
For each and every one!"

What is a Playground?

A playground is like a village
With all kinds of people there.
Some play ever so quietly
And others have energy to spare.

Some take rolls of leadership
And some swing high in the air.
While others sit on the sidelines
And at the activities, just stare.

But they all love when the bell rings
That signals that it's playground time.
And even though they are so different
They all play together, just fine!

Poems for the Classroom

School Librarian

We love to help you find a book
That especially speaks to you,
But we get a bit unhappy
When your books are overdue!

We will stamp your books correctly
With the due time and date.
And we really do not like it
When you return them late.

Don't dog-ear the pages
And keep them away from the pool.
To bring back a soggy book
Really isn't cool!

We love to have our books returned
In good shape and on time.
And if you disregard our rules
We will make you pay a fine!

So keep your librarian happy
And return those which are overdue
So that we will be able to enjoy the old ones
And have money for some new!

**How does one define
A Librarian?
We need more words
Or perhaps a few books!**

Taste of Paste

School Nurse

I can't kiss away your hurts like your mommy.
But she would want you to come to me.
If while you are on the playground
You fall and skin your knee.

She would want you to tell me
If your tummy aches.
Or you are feeling yukky
And your body has the shakes.

So if you are not well
Just tell me so.
And I will call your Mom
And let her know.

You can rest here with me
I will tend you and not forget you
Keeping you safe and sound
Until she can come and get you.

Our Janitor

You won't see litter in our schoolyard
For he keeps our school so nice and neat
And never will you see lying around
Stuff to trample under our feet!
He keeps the hallways shining
The floors are waxed just so
In fact our school looks pretty spiffy
Anywhere you go!!

We call him "Mr. Spiffy"!

Poems for the Classroom

With Gratitude

Mr. Cool

Thank you Mr. Wilson
For driving us to school.
We may not ever say it,
But we think you're really cool!

Thank You Bus Driver

There are no words of gratitude
Equal to the task you do.
So I'm hoping that this little gift
Will convey my heartfelt thanks to you!

To Our Janitor

Thank you Mr. Johnson
For everything you do.
Our school is clean and pleasant
Because of the diligence of you!

Cafeteria

Thank you Cafeteria ladies
For the work you do each day.
I know sometimes we are noisy
And get in the way.

But you always look up smiling
As we come through the door..
And never fuss at us
If we drop a tray onto the floor!

The Big Yellow Bus

Riding The Bus

Oh what fun to ride the bus
And go places far away!
I would love to ride the bus
And go to school each day!

Why can't the bus pick me up
And take me off to class?
Every day I watch for it
But it just goes right on past!

One day I got to get on board
And what a fun time I had!
When I get to ride it every day
I will be so glad!!

School Bus Driver

It's School Bus Driver Appreciation Week
And only once a year it comes
To recognize your dedication to your job
And your care of our little ones.

Although we only celebrate one week
In our hearts we know
That you deserve our thanks each day
And I just wanted to tell you so!

Bus Drivers Rule the Road!

Poems for the Classroom

I Drive the Bus

The mothers watch for me
As I rumble down the street.
I can almost hear
The patter of their children's feet.

They know that I'm getting closer
Than I was moments before.
And I'll be there to pick them up
So, they hustle out the door!

They line up at the corner
And some of the little ones are afraid.
But the bigger kids are giddy
Over all the new friends they've made.

At the first of the year
Some moms don't like me.
Because I take their little ones away
And they must do without them
For a very long and lonesome day.

But before the year is over.
They know that I'm a friend.
And by the end of summer.
They are ready for school to begin–again!

You looked so much bigger when I was short!

Retirement Poems

Retirement

Yesterday I was working so hard
That at the end of the day
I was exhausted and tired.

But today the sun can rise and set
And I can remember
Or I can forget.

I can get up if I've had enough sleep
Or go back to bed
And count some more sheep.

I can get dressed and go out
Or stay in my jammies all day
Clean my house or go out and play.

I can dine on peanut butter and jelly
Or toast and muffins
Or I can buy lunch and cook nuthin'.

Oh. how wonderful just adding a "RE"
In front of "Tired"
Can make your world be!!

Today The Sun Can Rise and Set
And I Can Remember
Or I Can Forget

Poems for the Classroom

As You Retire

As you retire from your profession
And enjoy a well earned rest.
Those you have helped along the way
Pray for you a retirement that is blessed.

May it be blessed with happiness, warmth and love.
And may there be wonderful opportunities for you
To reap the rewards of your dedicated labor
Doing the things you've always wanted to do.

You were always ready to help us
When we needed your expertise.
And you always did your best
To put our minds at ease.

You knew that our children
Were our source of concern and joy.
And you treated with such tenderness
Every single girl and boy!

We all watched you in various situations
As you so patiently and lovingly taught and tended
Each of your student charges
With the gentleness that God intended.

So it is with hearts full of gratitude
That we share this wonderful time with you.
And because of your wonderful giving spirit
We know that God's blessings will rain down on you.

You have been a wonderful Blessing for our children!

On Your Retirement

"Congratulations" and "Best Wishes"
Are lovingly sent your way,
To celebrate with you
This very special day!

You've worked hard for many years,
And done the best you could.
You handled everything that came your way
The bad things along with the good.

And now it's time to take a break,
And do things you want to do.
But no matter where this new path goes-
Our thoughts and wishes go with you!

Re-Tired

No, being tired yesterday
And being tired again today
Does not mean you are "retired!

A Retirement Farewell

Goodbye Tension!
Hello Pension

Putting "RE"
In Front of Tired
Makes a World
of difference!

Poems for the Classroom

A Few Years Ago

When I was just a kid in school,
I wrote with pen and ink.
I hadn't heard of computers
To help me write and think.

My memory was inside my head
And Meg was my best friend's name.
A megabyte did not exist
And a mouse had a Disney name!

I sat on the grass and looked up at the sky
And said words like "cool" and "groovy."
I bought my shoes at Tom McCann's
And wasn't very choosey!

But today I have a mouse
That sits upon my desk.
And when I want to write a poem
My laptop computer is the best!

I buy new memory every month or so
And my camera is now electronic.
And when I put a little disk inside,
It writes my photos upon it!

Years ago, a gigabyte I did not understand,
And had no idea what it could store.
I still don't understand the technicalities-
But I know I need some more!!

Taste of Paste

Congratulations

We knew this day was coming
And we thought we were prepared.
But our eyes are a little misty
As we think of all we've shared.

We have gone through lots of trying times
And had a lot of good times, too.
Among the memories we will cherish
Are our special memories of you!

So "Congratulations" as you leave
And know that although we must now part
We will always cherish those memories
And keep them in our hearts.

Retirement

We are all gathered here today
Because of something
We want to say-
Ms. Dee is retiring
And we all wish her the best.
And pray that with happiness
She will be blessed.
We want to thank her
For all that she has done
To make learning exciting
And filled with fun!

Poems for the Classroom

For My Co-Workers

I have such a wonderful time
Working here with you.
I enjoy the friendship
And the caring things you do!

You are all so kind and helpful:
You make working a blast.
And the friendships formed with all of you
I know will last and last.

When you see something funny
Or a silly e-mail comes in,
I like that you share with me
The things that make you grin!

But when there is a serious need
That someone has or sees around him
With genuine care and concern
Each person here surrounds him.

We are such a compatible group of folks
With like minds and attitudes.
And for all of my co-worker friends
My heart is filled with gratitude!

Friends

In my gallery of friends
Each of you come into view
Making me feel fortunate
To have friends like you.

Though we go our separate ways
And eventually all of us will part.
Memories of our happy times as classmates
Will linger in each heart.

So Sad to See You Go

It's been such fun
To work with you
And I'm sad to see you go.
But only by trying one's wings
Does a person ever grow!

So try your wings and soar!
We want the best for you.
We know that you will succeed
In anything you do!

So come back and visit us.
Don't stay away too long.
For we are your friends
And won't forget you
Even when you're gone.

Farewell to Co-worker

Congratulations and best wishes
On your new career opportunity!
We know that you will go far
And we can't wait to see.

Please know that you will be missed.
And we won't forget you here.
For even though you will be gone
In our hearts you will be near.

So long. Farewell.
Come see us now and then!

Poems for the Classroom

Thank You

In our daily workday world.
Sometimes it's hard to impart
All the love and gratitude
That's in our heart.
Sometimes there seems to be
No words to say
That you enrich our lives
And bless our day.
But with this little book.
Let us try to show you
Just how we really feel
As our feelings of friendship
And love we reveal.
This little book can only begin
To thank you for all you do
And most of all to express
Just how grateful we are for you!

Looking Back

I sit here with my memories
Of happy times in the past.
And although those days are over
The friendships made will last.
The hallways rang with our laughter
And the bell seemed to signal to all.
That memories were being made
Which we forever would recall.
So I close my book and smile
As I go back in my mind again.
To those friends that I made in yesteryears
And who each remain a treasured friend.

Early School Days

Mommy's First Day of School

Mommy went to school today
To take her baby boy.
With heart full of mixed emotions
None of them including joy!

Mommy went to school today
To take her little son.
With backpack on his little frame
He was quite the collegiate one!

Mommy went to school today
To check the teachers out.
Making sure they were nice and sweet
And didn't raise their voice or shout.

Mommy went to school today.
Second day in a row.
Leaving little one with "lubs."
It was so hard to go.

"Can you hear my heart breaking
Can you see inside my heart?
Can you feel the millions of kisses given
Before I tore myself apart?"

Tomorrow will be better
I just know that it will be...
Mommy is getting used to school
And so is he!

Poems for the Classroom

First Day of School (Son)

I had to drop my son off
For the first day of school today.
I watched him walk in the door
And knew that he must stay.

It was so hard to leave him
And trust that he would be
As safe in their protection
As he would be with me.

I trust they will treat him
With the utmost of care.
And I can hardly wait until
He is home with his day to share.

Somehow I will keep busy
And go on about my day...
Well, as soon as I get back into my car
And finally drive away...

First Day

A first day of school
Is such an important day.
Staying in our hearts and minds
Are things that our teachers say.
The way our teachers treat us
And the way we learn to respond
Stays in our memories
And those memories live on...

**The memories of this very first day—
In little hearts will forever stay**

Taste of Paste

First Day of Pre-school (Daughter)

My little baby girl
Smile on her face
Lost in the middle
Of mommy's tight embrace.

How can I leave her here
With people I don't know?
What will happen to my baby
When I have to go?

Will they treat my angel
With tenderness and care?
What about the other kids?
Will they know to share?

How can I stand it?
What will I do today?
How can I get back into my car
And how can I drive away?

I know you think I'm silly
I'm not like this as a rule.
Only on the morning
Of my baby's first day at pre-school!

**Look around you and you will see
Things that shape a memory!
So please do every thing you should
To make a memory that is good!**

Poems for the Classroom

Off To School

I am off to school today!
I am ready for my ride.
Looking forward to getting there
And to seeing what's inside.

I know that I will like it.
Can't wait to be on my way.
I will meet lots of new friends.
And see them every day.

There is my desk where I will sit
When I am at school each day.
I will study hard and do my work
And at recess I will play.

I know that at the end of day
My mom will come and get me—
I will not ever be concerned
That she might forget me.

Little Leora

My little Leora started school today...
Please if you see her...
Invite her to play!
Take care of my sweetie
And treat her with care
And if you have cookies
Invite her to share.

Taste of Paste

First Day of School Blues

I have to go to school tomorrow.
It isn't really my idea at all.
But they told me last summer
I had to start school in the fall.

I have circled it on the calendar
In a marker, bright and red.
Put a note on the refrigerator,
And laid out my clothes
By the side of my bed.

Guess there is no chance
Of Mom forgetting the date,
Or of my showing up absent
Or getting there late...

Looks like I must do it
So, education, I'm on my way!
Growing up gets more difficult
Every single day!

Goodbye to the Simple Life

I love being home with Mommy
And all the fun we have each day
I hate to think those times
Will suddenly go away.

I'm off to go to school.
To school, to school,
To school!

Poems for the Classroom

Baby's First Day of Pre-school

You brought your baby to school
And I saw the love in each face.
As you said goodbye to each other
With such a sweet embrace.

Yes, you can leave her here
With people you don't know.
And trust that she will be safe with us
When off to work you must go.

We will treat your little one
With tenderness and care.
And all of the other children
Equally our love will share.

We know how hard it is to do
What you had to do today.
How difficult to get back into your car
And then to drive away.

We don't think you're silly
And know that you're not like this as a rule.
But this is a very special red letter day-
Your little one's first day at pre-school!

Red Letter Day
Baby's Going to Pre-school!

Taste of Paste

Grandchild's First Day of School

God bless you little one
As you go to school today!
May God send His angels to watch over you
As you work and as you play!

It was not so very long ago
That I sent your Mommy off to school.
And she felt just the same as you do today
Being a bit nervous is not "uncool!"

If you should feel a little shy
Just think of your mom and me
For we are with you in your heart
Though you won't be able to see.

Just know that we love you
And want you to have life's best.
School is a great big wonderful step
That will get you to the rest!

So be off to school my little one
Enjoy your day and have lots of fun.
And we will be here waiting for you
When your first happy day is done!

School is Wonderful and fun Exciting days To laugh and run

Poems for the Classroom

Grandbaby Starts to School Today

It wasn't so very long ago.
In fact it seems like yesterday.
That I sent my baby off to school
And watched her as she walked away.

But time has so swiftly flown
And the years have passed away.
And no longer is it my child in line.
But my grandchild who starts school today.

God bless this tiny little child
Who stands so bravely ready to attend
Her very first school day today...
And Lord, please send her a special friend.

The Essence of Youth

What is the essence of youth?
What is that sweet perfume?
That only the young ones know?
What is the substance in their being
That gives them a special glow?
'Tis youth itself, that entity we seek
As in awe and reverence
About the essence of youth we speak.

So small now—
Life's just beginning

Taste of Paste

Your First Time On The School Bus

I looked for my shadow one morning
I looked almost everywhere!
When I finally remembered that
You would not be there!

My sweet smiling shadow
That made my day so sweet.
I had sent you off on the big yellow bus
That rumbled down our street!

Oh. how I hated that yellow bus
When it took you away...
But how I loved that bus
At the end of a very long day!

I could hardly wait to see my big girl
Who so bravely got aboard!
And throughout the day
You could hear me pray:
Oh. please protect her. Lord!!

And sure enough the bus came back
And brought you home to me.
And though it's been a few short hours.
It seemed like an eternity!

The Big Yellow Bus Comes Down My Street Honking It's Horn Just For Me!

Poems for the Classroom

First Day Blues

Today I watched you
As you got ready to leave.
And I admit a part of me
Began to gently grieve.

I knew the pain inside each of you–
The hurting in each heart.
This first time of separation
For two little ones never far apart.

But I watched you as you held the hand
Of your little sister there.
And in my heart so silently
I breathed a "thank you" prayer.

I am so happy to have this day recorded
To look at again and again.
When sisters were not just sisters
But when they realized they were friends.

Kisses To Go

Don't forget to kiss your child
Before you send them my way.
A child with the memory of your kiss
Always has a better day!
Don't forget to hug them tight
When you tuck them in at night.
Wake them with a smile next day
And leave them with happy thoughts
As you send them on their way!

Taste of Paste

One More Kiss

Mommy give me one more kiss
Before I go to school today.
And leave the imprint on my face
And I will let it stay.

It's not that I think it's cool
Or that it looks so smart,
It just reminds me throughout the day
Of the love that's in my heart.

I know that you love me mommy
And the kiss print makes the kiss so real.
It's something that I look at during the day
And your kiss I can still feel!

And someday when I'm a mommy,
I'll kiss my kids each day.
And leave my heart print on their face
In this very special way.

We Will...

Take care of your child
As if he were our own.
Keep him as safe
As if he were at home.

I'm going to school
To learn and play
Fun new things
I'll do each day!

Poems for the Classroom

Little Graduates' Mom

Today I watch as my darling
Earns a diploma from school.
Forgive me for being teary.
I'm not like this as a rule!

This is such a milestone-
One that tugs at a mommy's heart.
I have so many emotions
That I don't know where to start!

When did my baby grow up?
Where did my little one go?
What happened to the time?
Does anybody know?

I will treasure this moment forever
Along with special moments that come my way
The first in a long line of milestones
Her Kindergarten Graduation Day!!

For A Very Special Graduate

We have watched you through the years
Grow through laughter
And grow through tears.
You've learned so much
And grown in every way
And we are proud to honor you
On your special day!

Taste of Paste

Little Bitty Graduate

My eyes were teary
When I saw my baby girl
With dimpled cheeks
And baby curl
Walk proudly up to claim
The little diploma
That bore her name.
I'm sure there are grads
Of colleges and such
Whose degrees to them
Could mean as much.
But I felt my proud heart flip-flop
And truly thought that it would stop.
For I was so proud to be able to say
This is my baby's graduation day!

Your Special Day

We have watched you
Throughout this last year.
You were so brave
And showed no fear.
You jumped right in
And tried all things new
In a way that is so especially you!
You have learned so much
And grown in every way
And we are proud to honor you
On your special Graduation Day!

Poems for the Classroom

Precious Cargo

Our most valuable possessions
Are not transported by armored trucks
And guarded by security,
But are transported in school buses.

I Can Do

I can do some really great things
That only I can do
For I can make the special sound
That monkeys make at the zoo!

I can do some really fun things
Like swing way up high in the sky
So very far that I can see each car
That is out on the street driving by!

I can do some very smart things
That no one but me can do
I can add. subtract. and divide
And I know my "tables" too!

I can do some very exciting things
That I know are special to do
For I can dream my very own dreams
Only I know when they have come true!

The wheels on the bus
They come to my house
And take me to school
The wheels on the bus
Are oh, so cool!

Taste of Paste

Grade by Grade

First Grade
First grade is hard.
I thought it would be fun.
But there is so much to do.
And teacher says it must be done!

Hey! It's recess time
And my buddies won't wait!
I guess I've changed my mind-
First grade may be great!

Second Grade
I went to school last year
And learned to write and read
I don't think I should go to second grade
I think I've learned all I need!

In first grade. I learned my numbers
And all of my letters. too.
I don't see how second grade
Could teach me anything new!

But Mom says that I must
And so off to second grade I go
Won't they be surprised
At all the stuff I know?

<u>Poems for the Classroom</u>

Third Grade Blues

Last year I was in second grade
And I was so content
Because I learned so awfully much
I felt it was time well spent.

Today I am going to third grade
And I feel a bit afraid
For I have no earthly idea
What I will do in my new grade!!

Fourth Grade Is Fierce

One day the teacher said
We were going to multiply.
No longer can I be content to add.
I could not help but sigh!

So we multiplied two numbers
And found there are tables we can use.
Teacher said we'd learn more each day
Lest she would confuse!

Multiplication was not too bad
And in fact I was getting rather excited
But today the teacher said
These numbers must be DIVIDED!

Do I Know More Than I think I Know? Or Do I Think I Know More Than I Know?

Taste of Paste

Movin' Up

I loved being in the first grade.
I knew I could start out
Learning with my buddies
What school was all about.

Second grade was a bit harder
But I loved the things we did
I think I've got the hang of
Being an educated kid.

Third grade was very interesting
And there was new stuff every day
Along with brand new activities
And sports we got to play.

But I'm a little leery
Of what fourth grade will be
For everything in all of those books
Will be brand new to me!

A Big Kid Now

I am in the first grade
That means I'm a big kid now.
I can do all kinds of things
That before I didn't know how!

I can read and write a bit
And have met lots of friends
Every day there's more new stuff–
It seems that it never ends!

Poems for the Classroom

Fourth Grade

Fourth Grade is fun
It's the best grade yet!
But please remind me
If I should forget.

I have math homework
And I can't do it
And I wish for third grade
Because that's where I knew it.

So please remind me
That fourth grade is best
Especially right after
I get back my test.

Winners!

Winners don't whine
And whiners don't win
A whiner will be a loner
And drive away a friend.
Don't be a whiner
Or you will be ignorable
For most of us.
Find whining
To be deplorable!!

First Graders Are First Rate!

Taste of Paste

All Tied Up

(learning to tie my shoes)

All parents try to help kids learn
To tie their shoelaces in a bow.
It can be quite nerve-racking
As most every mother knows!

Yesterday I found my yarn
Tied in little knots.
Then I found my jogging shoes
All tied and lumped together in twos...

When I got out the big cotton mop,
I saw that all its little strands
Were knotted and jumbled together.
Was this done by little hands?

I paused a moment to consider
When I had such an awful fear.
Our hound dog ran across the room
Trying to protect his ears...

A picture is worth a thousand words they say. Wow! We must be worth millions!

Poems for the Classroom

I Can Tie My Shoes

I have a little poem
That I learned to say
And it helped me to learn
To tie my shoes today!

I know that I have to criss and cross
And go underneath the bridge.
But the part I can't get right...
Is making a loop or pulling it tight!

I know about the tail
But how to make the loop...
I forget about the wrapping part
I just can't get the scoop.

Hey, while I said the poem
Imperfect though it might be,
My fingers did the work
And tied my shoes for me!!!

Shoes like kids Can become Tongue-tied, dirty And all knotted up!

Taste of Paste

Best Buddies

We are more than playmates
The best of friends are we.
We are buddies forever
My big sis and me!

My big sis is so much fun.
We love to run and laugh and play,
And do such fun things together.
I love her more than words can say!

Although we are together
Each day as a rule...
She now fills her backpack
And heads off to school.

She holds my hand and gives me a hug
Before she has to go inside.
And I am so very glad
That mommy and me get to give her a ride.

I love taking her to school
And watching her go on her way,
For I know that soon she will be home
And once more we can play.

I got to go with her one day
And we packed a bag for me.
Because we are best of friends
And I wanted everyone to see.

We will be best friends forever
When we're as old as old can be.
And just like we are right now
My very best friend and me!

Poems for the Classroom

Staying At Home From School

At our house we have a rule.
A kid can't stay home from school.
Unless he's sick or almost dyin'.
There's no use in even tryin'!

A tummy ache keeps some kids free
But that doesn't work-no not for me!
Nor does an earache or throat that's sore
It has to be worse...oh so much more!

At our house we sometimes try.
And we may whine and we may cry.
But it is the general rule
A kid has gotta go to school!!

Our mom says school is good for us
And puts us on that yellow bus.
Whether it is raining, sleeting or snowing,
It's pretty sure that to school we are going!

She says that someday we will be glad
For all the schooling that we've had.
But for now I'd love a day
To skip school to stay home and play!!

A tummy ache keeps some kids free But that doesn't work no not for me!

Taste of Paste

As a Rule... (Kid)

I'm really quite happy as a rule.
Don't even mind the summer's end.
And the fact that it always means
We are going back to school.

I enjoy the excitement of it
And it always provides a bit of fun.
I like getting all new supplies
And the thought of seeing everyone...

But this year is different.
There is a sadness in my heart
As I face the school year
Knowing that my brothers and I will be far apart.

I know that they are excited
And I really and truly understand
That they must keep on growing
And they don't need to hold my hand.

But we have always been together.
And our house has been full of noise.
The kind that can only be attributed
To a group of teen-age boys.

It's the thought of our house being empty
And no noisy brothers and friends to enjoy
That makes it rather difficult today
To think I will be the only "at home boy!"

Poems for the Classroom

As a Rule...(Parent)
(for mom to put in son's book)

You don't seem to mind the summer's end
And are really quite happy as a rule
Even though it always means
That it's time to go back to school.

I know that you enjoy the excitement of it
And it always provides a bit of fun.
You like getting all new supplies
And the thought of seeing everyone...

But this year is different
I see a sadness in your heart
As you face the school year
Knowing that your brothers and you will be far apart.

I know that they are excited
And that you understand
That they must keep on growing
And you don't need them to hold your hand.

But you have always been together
And our house has been full of noise
The kind that can only be attributed
To a group of teen-age boys.

It's the thought of our house being empty
And no noisy brothers and friends to enjoy
That makes it rather difficult today
For you to realize you will be
The only "at home boy!"

Taste of Paste

Things Mom Should Know

I didn't want to go to school today
You would think Moms would know
That kids don't want to go to school
If there's new fallen snow!
I didn't want to eat my dinner
No kid wants veggies to eat
When there is left over cake
Or something else that's sweet.
I told my Mom some of these things
To help her understand my view
But I found out that moms of kids
Have their own ideas
Of just what kids should do...

Girls Versus Boys

Girls are much more fun than boys
And if I had my way
I'd tell the schools to invite such girls
And send the boys away!
Boys tease us and harass us
And hold spiders in the air
Right in front of dainty little girls
Just to give us a scare.

**I love new crayons
in colors so bright.
A box of one hundred is a delight!**

Poems for the Classroom

Rules and Report Cards
Too Many Rules

I had to go to school today
But they didn't let us play!
They made us listen to all they said
When I wanted to play instead!

The teacher told us
What we couldn't do
She had listed a million rules
Before she was through!

I knew all kinds of brand new games
And learned all of the new kids' names.
But teacher came and rang a bell
And had us do a "show and tell."

But when you share
You only talk for a minute
And there's one little room
And you must stay in it!

There's all kinds of neat stuff outside
A few swings and also a slide.
But inside is where I have to stay
For most of the whole school day!

All in all school might be nice
If I could go just once or twice
But how can it be really cool
If I have to obey every RULE!

93

Taste of Paste

Boys

Boys are much more fun than girls
And if I had my way
I'd tell the schools to change their rules
And send all the girls away!

Girls have no sense of humor
About things that boys find fun
But I'll have to change my mind someday
'Cause I'll have to marry one!

Seat Chart Blues

Girls are gross
And yukky and silly
I'd much rather sit
By Larry or Billy
But teacher put me here
And I must stay
Sitting by a girl
And miserable all day!

I hate being charted
It's not my style
I think I will sit here
And pout for awhile
HEY! That new kid
Looks awfully neat
And look she is sitting
Right next to my seat!

Poems for the Classroom

Girl's Seat Chart Blues

Teacher gave us all a chart
To show us where to sit
I wanted to sit by my best friend
Because I have not done that yet.
But here I am by a boy
And do not know his name
But this is what the chart shows
So, I'm stuck here just the same!

Seating Chart

Today I passed out the seating chart
And posted one on the wall
So that you would see it
And know that it was fair for all.
Some students need to be up front
So the board they can see better
And not have to squint their eyes
To make out every letter.
Others may want to sit
By a buddy or a pal
But I think each one of you should
Make friends with each guy and gal.
So do not panic if you see
You are by someone you do not know
But take the opportunity today
A new friend to get to know!

Taste of Paste

Report Card Blues...

The teacher called us to her desk
And talked to us about our tests.
And then she made my life so hard...
When she handed me my...report card!

"Take this home and get it signed
And bring it back to me."
I peeked inside the envelope
To see just how bad it would be!

"Oh no!" I squealed in disbelief
When I saw what I had done
There was an ugly grade on it...
But at least it was only one!

I thought about my options
And considered report card crime...
Altering via computer
But didn't want to do the "time."

'Cause surely I would be detected
And do time alone in my room
With no TV or videos for comfort.
I could not stand the gloom!

So I wait here for my parents
And I know what they will do
They will take away my Internet
So I bid farewell to you...

Look what I did, Mom!

96

Poems for the Classroom

Report Card Day

The kids don't know that teachers
From bad report cards get no thrill
But it is a task that we must do
To show their progress that is real.

I'm sure that on report card day
They hope we get the flu
But we show up and spoil their dreams
For that's what teachers do!

Learning Is Fun

And I've just begun!
And today is an important day
Today Kindergarten
Tomorrow first grade
Look out world
I'm on my way!

Look out world
I'm on my way!
My Dad will be proud
I made one A
No D's or F's
Just C's and B's
Time to shout
Hey, look at me!

97

Taste of Paste

The Dreaded F

I am sad and distraught
I am beside myself
For I know that on my paper
I will receive an "F" !

I turned my paper in too fast
I should have waited longer
And maybe by then
My brain would've been much stronger.

But I hurried to the teacher's desk
And placed my paper there
Walking away with heavy heart–
Oh life can be so unfair!

So, now I wait to see the score
That teacher gave to me
Praying hard with all my might
That I might get a "D" !

Here she comes and with a smile
(Oh how can she be so cruel)
She places the paper next to me
And oh my stars! I got a "B" !

A = $10.00

B =   5.00

C =   1.00

D =   .25

F=TROUBLE!!!

<u>Poems for the Classroom</u>

Summer Vacation

The Classroom is Empty

The classroom is empty
All the students have left today
School is out for the summer
And they have all gone home to play.

The board once filled with lessons
And the chairs that held boys and girls
Are empty now and look lonesome
Not part of summer worlds.

The teacher's desk looks so big
Standing so tall and aloof
Quietness overwhelms the room
Where sometimes rowdiness raised the roof.

Look around and enjoy the feeling
Of emptiness and silence that is fleeting
For soon again the classroom will be filled
Up to the maximum seating!

Filled Up

A classroom is never really empty, it is filled
With all of the hopes and dreams of students
Who once filled the seats and the pride of
Teachers who urged them on to recognize those dreams!

Learning is more fun when the school day is done!

Taste of Paste

Back to School

End Of Summer

Summer is over
And it's back to school
I don't mind it
As a general rule.
I have tasted the freedom
That comes with the summer sun
But I welcome the thrill
Of the new year just begun.
So bring on the books
And bring on the learning
And by mid-winter
For Summer I will be yearning!

Summer Come Back

Summer, summer, summer
Where did you go?
It is only September
And I miss you so!
I know that you will come again
But it can't be too soon!
How can I wait all year long
For the month of June!

Notebooks, pen's and pencils, Markers, paste and ink— Time to learn to think!

Poems for the Classroom

Where Did Summer Go?

Where oh, where, did summer go?
I asked my mom,
But she didn't know.
She didn't seem sad
That fall was coming.
Just last night
I heard her humming!

Why oh, why, is vacation ending
Why must I end the free time I'm spending?
I asked my dad
And he didn't seem to know
But gave me money for a picture show.

Why, oh why, must school start tomorrow?
My face wears a frown
And my heart is in sorrow
I asked my teacher
And she understood my pain.
She didn't know why tomorrow
The school year must start again!!

Summer, summer
Where did you go?
It's time for school
Do I have to go?

Taste of Paste

Classroom Traditions

Measuring Students Each Year

Teacher measured us today
And I'm getting really tall.
I think that of all the feet in class
Mine are the biggest of them all!

My hands are growing bigger
And can hold so much more stuff
Overall. I'd say I'm perfect-
Just exactly big enough!

Growing

I had a special playmate
Who had to move away.
I miss him in the summer
For that's when we got to play.

He's going to come and visit us
And I don't want to hurt his feelings
So I'll try not to look
For his mom told mine just yesterday that
He has grown another foot!

Overall. I'd say I'm perfect—
Just exactly big enough!

Poems for the Classroom

How Fast A Child Can Grow

Whether it is sunny
Or whether it is snowing
Children may be standing still-
But they are growing!
Little feet are getting bigger
Hands are holding more
Legs are getting longer
And arms wrap around you more.
Sometimes it's hard to understand
Just how fast a child can grow
That's why I measure them each year
So all of us will know!

Growing Fast

Teacher measured us today
And I'm getting bigger
I'm proud to say!
I'm taller now than I was before
And I've grown so much taller
That my legs are sore!
My handprint is much larger too
And my feet don't fit in last year's shoes!
I think that it is fun to be
This older and bigger size of me!!

Taste of Paste

School Photos

In this book. I've gently placed
Your school photos
And they are very special ones
For they are the first such photos
Of the many yet to come.

Posing with your classmates.
You look so grown up and proud.
The picture brings me to nostalgic tears
(But mommies are allowed.)

The next page holds your own photo.
Taken just of you
I love the school boy look of it—
It is a cherished thing to view.

I love knowing that I can document each year
With photos of both you and your class.
It gives us something to look back on
To remember school friends of the past.

I'm saving places in your book
For photos yet to be.
And each year your school photos
Will be very special to me.

Picture Perfect— Say Cheese!

Poems for the Classroom

Photo Day Note to Parents

Dear Parents:
We are having photos made
And want your child to look their best.
Please see that their hair is combed
And they are neatly dressed.

We will do all we can
To keep them looking spiffy
By having the photographer come early
And snap them in a jiffy!

So please tell them no bunny ears
Or making funny faces, please.
So that all of us who are in charge
Can get through this day with ease.

Your Photos

I look at the photo of your first day of school
And my heart causes my eyes to tear.
For here in my hand is another photo
A photo of you in your senior year!

I cannot believe that I hold in my hand
A photo of you so handsome and grown.
I knew that the years would quickly fly by
And soon you would be on your own.

But now I hold in my hand
The evidence that this is so true.
And for each one I place in your book
My heart holds that memory, too.

Taste of Paste

Photo Phobia

I always get into trouble
When it's photo day.
I don't really mean to
And I don't plan it that way.

I hate to pose for photos
So I do some silly stuff—
Like making silly bunny ears
Until my teacher says "ENOUGH!"

And sometimes I get by with it.
No one sees me make a face
Until Mom gets the pictures back—
And then I am in disgrace!

Photo Day

I'm all dressed up
Ready for school
I don't look this spiffy
As a rule
But today is photo day
And mom said I had to dress this way!

(Last page of album)
What an exciting educational journey
This has been for you
With photos from those very first years
And now you have made it through.
As you looked back upon the photos
Placed upon each page with care
Know that a loving heart
Gently placed them there.

Poems for the Classroom

Gift Album Poem

Sometimes it's hard to impart
All the love and pride
That's in our heart.

Sometimes there seems to be
No words to say
That you make my life
And bless my day!

But with this little book
Let me try to show,
That I love you more
Than you'll ever know.

You bring me joy
And I'm so proud of you
And will be forever
Our whole lives through!

Special Things

If you wonder if it is worth it
To do special things for the students you teach.
All you need to do is look back
At your school years and what was special to you.

School Daze...
Memories of the Past

Taste of Paste

Remember When

I look back at photos
From when I was a kid,
And think of all the fun
And wonderful things I did.

I remember my school days
As I see these folks today,
Even though I'm an adult
And not a kid at play.

It does not surprise me
That the folks I looked up to then,
I still look up to today
As I remember when.

Your Portraits

Each year they took a photo
From the time you entered school,
And your parents always bought them
It was a family rule.
I've gathered them all together here
And put them in a book,
And now from Kindergarten to Graduation
At your school years you can look.

**I look back at photos
from when I was a kid,
And think of all the fun
and wonderful things I did.**

Poems for the Classroom

Teen Life

Zit

On my face is a horrible zit,
It goes on and on
And just won't quit!

Why oh, why did this happen to me?
Why not on my arm
Or on my knee?

I went to bed looking fine
And woke this morning
With this zitty design!

Prom

Lovely princess in a beautiful gown,
Beautiful young lady
Out for a night on the town.
Precious teenage daughter
Mom and Dad's pride and joy
How hard it is to place our a princess
Into the care of a teenage boy!!

All Grown Up

Look out teachers, here they come-
Your students looking all grown up today
But they will be back as themselves tomorrow
When their finery is all put away...

109

<u>Taste of Paste</u>

Graduation Girl

Today is a new beginning.
A new adventure starts today.
And I know that you will handle it
In your customary, wonderful way!

I've watched you from the time
You were an infant small
To your graduation day
As you stand so proud and tall.

I watched you through babyhood
And loved you till I thought my heart would burst.
As you went through hits, bites and bruises
(Which hurt me the worst.)

I've nursed you through illness
And applauded you through awards and such
And in every moment of your life
I've been aware of your special touch.

God has granted this mother's prayer
And has done what I asked Him to
He gave me the greatest gift I could ever desire
When He gave me you!

No parent could ever be
Prouder of their daughter
Than I am of you every day.
For you measure in your heart
Everything you do and say.

continued...

Poems for the Classroom

...continued from previous page

You grades are not what makes me proud
Or the wonderful things you always seem to do
The things that stir this heart of mine
Is the inner strength, love and beauty that is you!

So, go out dear lovely daughter,
And meet life's challenges each day.
Continue to be the person you are
And may God always lead your way.

And remember when you need me
I will be close at hand
To help and guide and listen
For I'm your biggest fan!

To Our Son

You have gone through the system
And made the grade
You studied your lessons
And passed all your tests
At some things you excelled
And at others you did your best.
And now here you are
Diploma in your hand
Ready to go charging ahead
And I want to say
On this special day
You still never learned to make your bed!!
But congratulations anyway from Mom and Dad!

All Grown Up
and Charging Ahead!

Taste of Paste

For the Graduate

We have watched you through the years
Grow through laughter
And grow through tears.
You've learned so much
And grown in every way
And we are proud to honor you
On your special day!

Look Out World

Look out world
Here they come.
The products of
This year's graduation!

Look out world!
They're headed your way–
This group of students
Who graduated today!

Treat them kindly world
For this is all brand new
They're armed with education
And a new diploma, too!

Celebrate

Graduation is met
With elation and celebration—
(And that is just by the folks who sell the rings,
The invitations, rent the limos, sell the dresses!)

Poems for the Classroom

Prom Girl

(Alone at prom)

Sometimes things don't turn out
Exactly as we planned.
Sometimes we have to do the best
And just try to understand.

A Prom is such a special time—
A young girl's dream come true.
I look forward to my date
And of my Prom night...that's true!

But sometimes a modern girl
Has some quick decisions to make.
And I had fun even being just ONE
And being my own Prom DATE!

Night On The Town

Sixteen year olds in a limo
Going out for a night
On the town
The boys may be
Wearing sneakers
While the girls are
Dressed In gowns!

Prom Night—
Kids stay up partying.
Parents stay up worrying...

Taste of Paste

Senior Graduation Thoughts

Someday I will look back on this time
And it will be in my past
But for now it's in my present
And I want these moments to last.
For now our journey has just started
Our paths loom straight ahead
We will soon become the leaders
And will lead where once we were led.

Kids R Sick

Go Away Sickie Bugs

Go away sickie bug
Don't bother me again
Fly away in the air
Be gone with the wind!
I don't like germs
I don't like bugs
So fly away
Go to the moon
But stay away from me
And my room!

Feeling Yukky

I'm feeling awful!
Feeling just yukky
Mommy, please hug me
'Cause I'm one sick puppy!

Poems for the Classroom

Sicky

I woke this morning
And felt like a mess
What is wrong with me
I can't even guess!
I need a bunch of hugs
And lots of kisses, too.
Before the sickies leave me
And I feel brand new!

Chicken Spots!

I have the Chicken Pops!
I'm all broke out in chicken spots
And even though I itch a lots
No one can even see.
Except for my little nosey spot
And the tiny tosey spot
All my bestest rosy spots
Are covered up with clothes!
So how will I ever show my spots
To all my buddies (I have lots)
Who want to see my chicky pops
Through all these layers of clothes I've got?
I'm sitting on the biggest spots
Of all the biggest spots I've got
And these are the spots
That I can never show.
So now I sit and itch and scratch
My tosey spot and spotty back
And wait until that spot free day
When once again I'm free to play!

I Got Sick At School

I got sick at school today,
And I was really scared,
For even though I am seven
I was not prepared!
I had a fever in my head
And my tummy was full of aches,
My legs felt awfully wobbly
And every part of me had the shakes!
My teacher came and took my hand
And led me to the door
Of our own school nurse
And said that's what nurses were for!
She took my temperature
And had me rest a while,
And even though I felt awfully bad
I knew I had to smile.
No longer was I frightened
And I knew I need not worry,
Soon my mom came after me
For they called her in a hurry,
She took me home right to my bed
And said I had the flu,
But fortunately for Mom and me
The nurse had known what to do.
So, I guess I did the right thing after all
And I am no longer scared
Of getting sick when I'm at school
Because now I am prepared!

Poems for the Classroom

Sharing

If I have a cookie.
You have one. too.
For I will share
My cookie with you.

If you have a tummy ache.
I feel your pain
Until it is all better
And you are well again.

If you are happy.
Then I am glad.
When you are feeling down.
Then I am very sad.

Why do I feel this way
And do the things I do?
It's because we're friends
And I will always share with you!

Everyone is Ill at Our House

I had the measles.
Sister had the mumps.
Brother broke out in hives
With great big ole lumps!

Daddy had the flu
And the dog has fleas.
And I think my Mommy's getting sick
Because I just heard her sneeze.

<u>Taste of Paste</u>

The Teacher Snoozed at Me

Today my teacher had a runny nose
And it was as red as a big ole rose.
Mine was the desk she unfortunately chose
When she suddenly snoozed and snoozed!

Oweeeee!!!

OUCH! I fell and bumped my head
And Sue stepped on my toes.
Someone jabbed me with their elbow
And hit me in the nose!

My head hurts from thinking
And my ears are buzzing too
And it's only 9 am
On the first day of school!

Sticks and Stones

Can break your bones
And words can harm the spirit.
Put a watch over what you say,
Because little ears may hear it!

Dear Teacher

Suzee won't be in today
She woke up full of spots
We think she may be contagious
And have the chicken pox!

Poems for the Classroom

Seasons and Weather

What is As Lovely As Spring?

What is as gentle and lovely
As a day in Spring?
You are gentler and lovelier
And flowers you bring!
I love the feeling
Of being outdoors
And I love watching sunbeams
Dancing on floors.
I love Winter and Summer
And I don't mind Fall
But of all of the seasons
I love Spring best of all!

Tulips

There is magic in the tulip
More than any other flower.
It has a special glow
And a special kind of power.
Oh, how I love the tulip
And the beauty that it brings.
It adds sunshine to the morning
And freshness to our Spring.
I have often wondered
But I guess nobody knows
Why the tulip doesn't speak of love
Instead of the red, red rose.

Taste of Paste

More on Spring

What blooms will you bring
Lovely season of Spring?
What products of sheer delight
Can you add to my life?
Oh, I can hardly wait
For your opening date.
So hurry Spring
Please don't be late!

Spring

Thank you Lord
For beautiful Spring!
It is so special to me.
Watching the earth
Come back in rebirth
Reminds me of
Your gift to me!

Playing in the Snow

Come outside
In the snow and play
And let's make angels
For fun today!
Lay down in the snow
And flap your wings
And we will look like
Angel beings!

Poems for the Classroom

Snow

People in the tropics
Will never know
The fun it is
To play in the snow!

I love the feel of new fallen snow
Drifting by my face.
I love the look of flakes
Like bits of dainty lace.

I love waking in the morning
To see snow all around
Covering up the streets
And every patch of ground!

I love the thrill of walking
With those I love
Hand in hand.
And glove in glove!

I love to wear brand new boots
Cause last years just won't fit
Oh how I love the snow
Every part of it!!

Snow Angels

Little Angel in the snow
Looks just like someone we know...
Oh my goodness! Now I see
The little snow angel is ME!

Taste of Paste

Snow Friend Like You

What fun it is to build
A friend with which to play.
He will stand close by your side
And never move away!

What fun to decide on
What he will wear
On the shape of his nose
And the kind of hair!

You can make him tall
And make him thin
You can undo his figure
And start over again!

You can dress him in a dapper way
Or like a kid going out to play!
You can give him a scarf and hat
Or a baseball mitt and a wooden bat!

But just one thing
You must know
Your friend will melt
In the sun's warm glow!

My Umbrella

My umbrella is blue
And is brand spankin' new.
Ready to go with me.
Its first rain to see!

Poems for the Classroom

Snowman Soup

Good friends, good fun, good treats
In sunny or snowy weather-
Share a bit of chocolate
And celebrate being together.
Candy canes and kisses
Are good for anytime
And I'm so happy to share them
With special friends of mine!
So mix a bit of chocolate drink
And pop in a marshmallow or two,
And soon your snowman soup
Will make you feel warmer through and through!
You must share your Snowman soup
For that's how it was meant to be
You can't just share with one person
But pass along the same treat to THREE!

Rain

When I go outside
In the rain
To wear a raincoat
Is a pain.
But an umbrella
Can be lots of fun
It keeps out the rain
Until its done.
I love to go walking in the rain
And hear the splashing sound
Of the great big droplets
Splashing as they hit the ground.

Taste of Paste

Walking in the Rain

The raindrops splash
All around
Landing on my face
And on the ground.

They get me wet
From head to toe
And when I walk
My footprints show.

My eyelashes drip
And drops slide down my nose.
Only my big old boots
Keep water from my toes!

But even as I walk
And look up toward the sky.
While the outside of my nose is wet.
The inside of my nose is dry.

So. I have a silly question
Though I wish it were profound-
Do you suppose that
We would drown.
If God had built our noses

Upside
Down

?

Poems for Special Kids

My View

My view of the world
May be different than yours,
For you stand on two sturdy feet,
While I see the world from a different view.
I see it from a wheelchair seat!

But I see the world and I love what I see
And I love sharing my world with you.
For I don't fret and won't ever forget
That you are the best of my view!

I may see the world from a seat that's low
And peer through bars at places I can't go.
But I always see and recognize
The love for me that is held in your eyes.

I hope someday to see the world
From taller and stronger frame.
But until that dream comes true
I love looking at the world with you
And I love it just the same!

-For Baylee

I see the world and I love what I see, and I love sharing my world with you.

Taste of Paste

Mommy Had to Come to School

Mommy had to come to school today
To explain to my teachers one by one
Why I can't play at recess
And that I'm too weak to run.

I'm at a brand new school
And I really want to fit in.
Don't want to be left out.
No. I don't want that to happen again.

I wish that I were strong and well
And the playground I could share.
But instead while others play
I must watch them from a chair.

If I were on crutches
Or a wheelchair don't you know.
You would make allowances for me
But you just think I'm slow.

I look just like everyone else
But my body is out of whack.
It just doesn't give me what I need
There's so much that I lack.

So when you see a kid like me
Who isn't joining in the play.
Take the time to find out about them
And their fears help to allay.

You will be their hero
And will be remembered in a special way.
As the one who understood
And gave them a brighter day.

Poems for the Classroom

The Words in My Heart

The words in my mind are clear as day.
But when I try to say them to you
There may be a bit of delay.
And you may not understand the words that I say.

The words on my lips are formed perfectly
And I know exactly what I want them to be.
So don't judge me unkindly or think I don't know
What I want to say if my wording is slow.

The words in my heart are plain as can be
I wish that everyone who knows me could see
And hear as clearly as I
The words in my heart as speak them I try.

God hears my words and He gave them to me
And when I pray to Him, I speak perfectly.
For He sees in my heart each word I say
And understands perfectly each prayer I pray.

Just Watching

I wish that I were strong and well
And the playground I could share
But instead while others play
I must watch them from a chair.

I'm Just Like you—But Different!

Taste of Paste

My World is Different

My view is from down low
I see things from a different perspective
Everywhere I go.
I see things while I'm sitting down
Or when I'm lying prone.
But my heart sings and I have wings
When I'm all by myself alone.
In my imagination, I run and skip
And see the world as you do.
But during my waking hours
My legs restrict my view.
I'd like to see the world
From a taller and sturdier frame
And perhaps hear a softball coach
Call on me by name.
I'd like to stand on tippy-toes
And perhaps someday I will
For now I peek through life's bars
And view things while seated, still.
But my view is filled with awesome things
That sometimes you may not see.
For sometimes a lower viewing spot
Is a very good place to be.
I love my view and love my world
And each day it will get better.
For having family that loves me so much
Is what really truly matters!
I am just the same as you
The only difference is my view!

—For Baylee

Poems for the Classroom

We Are Alike

I saw the little one in a wheelchair
Ride out to the playground today
I saw the wistfulness in her eyes
And I knew that she longed so to play.

The kids were tossing the ball
And she watched as it went to and fro
I knew in my heart what she wanted to do
And I knew where she wanted to go.

The other kids ran about on legs big and strong
With arms that were muscular and tan
While this little one in a wheelchair
Reached out one small fragile hand.

But surprises and miracles happen
And the ball that had been tossed in the air
Somehow came right to her space
And found her sweet hand waiting there!

Oh. the smile on her face was priceless
And no equal to her joy have I seen!
For this moment she was playing
And she was a part of a team.

A young boy ran over to get it
And he gave her a wink and grin.
Before she handed it to him
And he ran off once again.

It takes only a moment
And only a step or two out of our way
To include those who need us
In the excitement of the every day!

Taste of Paste

(Response to "We Are Alike")
We are alike more than we are different.
We are the same more than we are not.
We have the same hopes and dreams-
The same plans and wants.
And those things with illness do not stop.

Losing an arm or leg doesn't take away your need
To hear someone say that you're their friend.
A leg that no longer works doesn't ever
Mean your fun loving days must come to an end.

A voice box that cannot make sounds
That people can understand.
Doesn't mean that you no longer need
To feel the touch of a loving hand.

Eyes that wear thick glasses
And can barely see to read.
Don't indicate that reading help
Is all that you will want or need.

Each heart reaches out for compassion
And waits so longingly.
Whispering to those who would listen
Please. someone. include me.

Four Eyes

Kids were teasing me today
And thought they'd make me run away.
But I fooled them all
Because to me
I am thankful for my extra "eyes"
For with them I can see!

Glasses

I got something new today
To help my eyes to see.
How lovely the world about me is
And the folks so dear to me!

I got something new today
That I wear to help me see-
I got brand new glasses
And the world is much clearer to me!!

I can see the leaves on the tree
As each individual leaf.
Not all jumbled up together-
What a grand relief!

The sky looks so much bluer now
And the grass such a lovely greenish shade
I love looking at the lovely world
What a difference my glasses have made!

Not Seeing Was Worse

I thought I could take teasing
That it wouldn't bother me.
I knew I could tolerate it
For now I can finally see!
But nobody said a single thing
Or teased a tiny bit.
And so I am happy with my new glasses
Which are a perfect fit!

I Can See

Look at me!
Now I can see!
Do you think the kids
Will laugh at me?

Will they point their fingers
At the specs on my face
And make me feel
That I'm in disgrace?

Will they call me "four eyes"
And ask me something lame.
Like. "Hey Suzee. did you know
That you've been "framed?"

Will they giggle and laugh
And tell each other I look strange
And whisper bad things
When I'm out of hearing range?

Well. I don't think so
But I'm not going to worry
'Cause finally I can see my friends
And they're no longer blurry!

**I don't mind wearing
whatever I need
for if I can see and hear-
then I can succeed!**

Poems for the Classroom

Un-braced And Free At Last

How much time has it been?
How many months have passed?
Happily now my braces are off
And I'm free at last!
Look out chocolate!
Look out gum!
Look out Hot Tamales!
Here I come!!

Braces

For ten years I was able
To eat, drink and chew
Anything I wanted...
Just like you.
Now I am getting braces
That will cover my teeth
And will curb my eating
And affect my speech!
I will accept the challenge
And do the best I can.
But exactly what the purpose is
I'm not sure I understand!

**Braces and glasses
and hearing aids, too,
Are just things created to
help people like you.**

Lessons to Learn

Math Can't Hurt

Students I hear you–
I hear you every day
As you make your frantic pleas
That mathematics would go away.

You say you liked addition,
And subtraction was just fine.
Multiplication is almost bearable,
But division blows your mind.

You say that you dread high school
Because Algebra looms ahead,
That you have nightmares about Geometry
While sleeping in your bed.

Don't let math intimidate you
Or cause you to feel sad
For once you understand it
Math really isn't bad.

Now that I've had my say
And my thoughts I've said
I must add that math can't hurt you
It is only in your head.

While Visions Of Numbers Danced In My Head

Poems for the Classroom

I Love To Teach Math

I teach Math because I love it
And I love what I can do
With numbers on a page
And what they can mean to you.

I only wish, in students, I could instill
A liking for Math that is for real
For this important subject so many abhor
But it is one that I absolutely adore

Gozinta

I learned a secret
About math today
And I created a game
That I like to play.

I choose a random number
And then I choose another
And figure out how many times
One gozinta the other!

Don't let math intimidate you
Or cause you to feel sad
For once you understand it
Math really isn't bad.

Taste of Paste

I Hate Math

I hate Math so much
I hate it with a passion
I don't mind addition
But I abhor subtraction!

Multiplication is way too hard
And long division makes me ill
Fractions give me a headache
And decimals are a pill!

I hate Math sincerely
I really, really do
If holding my breath would make it go away,
I'd hold my breath 'til I was blue!

I don't know why I have to take it
When I hate it with passion so true
But I see no way out of it-
So what is a kid to do!

Not Made for Math?

I don't think I'm made for math
For no matter what I do.
I can't get the answers right
Before my homework is due.
My brain tries to grasp the concept
And I make my numbers neat.
But I fear that mathematics
May soon be my defeat.

Poems for the Classroom

Loving Math

You might think of us as fanatics
Who love the very word—Mathematics
But though I might tend to agree
Math is very special to me!

I love the way Math never lies
You just need to know the 'how' and 'whys'
To understand the answer that you get.
And then the way to a solution—
Next time you won't forget.

I love the way a simple number
Can do so many things...
Can be used to create and investigate
And excitement it can bring.

Some people favor languages
Others love Science or History
But of all the subjects I could teach
Math was the only one for me!!!

Mathematically Speaking,
I'm 100% Sure
That I was 40% wrong
50% of the time
on the test...
if that is possible?

Taste of Paste

Master Artist

The teacher glanced at the offering
That a little child had brought.
A picture of the sky—
It was approval that she sought.

"How lovely." the teacher said.
And touched the sweet ones cheek.
But in truth she thought the talent
Of this one was really weak!

The sky wasn't sky blue at all.
And there were no distinguishing lines.
There were wild and vivid pinks and blues...
And nothing well defined...

She praised the child for what she had done
And in her heart she thought
That this one would do much better
Once she had been taught.

And then one day the teacher rose
And got an early start
And looking toward the sky.
She saw the little child's art.

Perfectly Designed by the Master's Hand!

Poems for the Classroom

God's Artwork

God doesn't color
Within the lines;
His colors aren't subdued.
His artwork on earth and sky
Is the loveliest to be viewed.
Let the beauty
Which God bestows.
On this earthly realm.
Remind you that
On this ship called life.
God is at the helm!

What a Gift

What a great and special gift
God gave us in color!
What a glorious sight to behold.
Colors soft and beautiful. colors bright and bold!
What beauty God gave us in nature
In each piece of grass or in each leaf.
So wonderful is sun or rainbow
To give our eyes such sweet relief!
What joy God gave us in each other
Each person whether great or small.
Each one is a precious masterpiece
For God is the creator of them all!
Look around you and enjoy the sunshine
As well as the rain. the snow or sleet
Find nature's artwork all around you
For each of His creations is unique!

Taste of Paste

Work Of Art

I had to smile when I saw you
With your drawing on your paper
And then on your legs as well
Where the paper ended. I couldn't tell!

It made me think for a moment
How wonderful God.
The original artist
Created the work that is you!

You are a masterpiece
Lovely in concept and design
Perfect in every way
Precious child of mine!

God's Art Is Everywhere

There is beauty everywhere
If you take the time to look
It can be found in little things
That will never be in a book.

It may be the sound of a whippoorwill
Singing in a tree.
The beauty of the hummingbird.
Or a busy little bee.

But God has filled the world
With incredible things to see
If you will just make the time
And use each opportunity!

Poems for the Classroom

Being Different And Being ME

Even as a child
I knew I was different
I knew I had to be
The individual that was me!

I could not stand
To always color within the lines
To create a flower
Or a leaf or vine.

It sometimes caused me problems
That failure to conform
But somewhere within my heart
A true artist was born.

No teacher could stifle me
Or cause me to pause
Should I desire a purple elf
Or a bright green Santa Claus!

And though I was misunderstood
With my artwork so wild and free.
Today I'm considered creative
And people copy me!

I'm as happy as happy can be
Being different
I'm just being
ME!

Taste of Paste

Musically Speaking

I love music—
I want a drum!
Mom says they are noisy.
Sis says they are dumb.

But I love the drum
And I love it's sound.
And everyone can hear me play
For miles and miles around!

What Instrument?

I want to play an instrument.
I want to play it well.
Will I someday be a musician?
Only time will tell.

I love all of the instruments
Which one is best I do not know.
So for now I'm just content
To play the radio!

Drum de Dum Dum

Banging, clanging
Loud as can be.
Drumsticks moving
So very quickly.
Hitting, striking
Making lots of noise.
That's why drums
Appeal to boys!

Poems for the Classroom

Music Lover

I'm a music lover
I listen to music every day
I hear music everywhere-
I hear it in my child at play!

I love music of every kind
As a mother and a wife
I love the sound of living-
The music of daily life.

I love the sound the piano makes
And I love to hear a drum
I love the sound of shoes on the walkway
When I hear my children run!

I love to hear the birds sing
And to hear a doggie bark
I love the sound of giggling kids
Playing in the park.

Oh. yes. I'm a music lover
Although I can't play a note
I can enjoy the wonderful music
That God through nature wrote!

Music

Let's talk about music
Let's make some musical sounds
Let's find musical instruments
That nature has placed all around!

Taste of Paste

My Computer Woes

I have a new computer,
As powerful as they come.
My dad bought it for me
Just because I am his son.

He told me not to crash it
Or get a virus on the drive.
And if I disobey him,
I hope I will survive.

It's just that I had one last year
And one the year before.
But of the time they last for me
My Dad is keeping score.

So I'm not downloading music
And treating it so tenderly.
For I think this is the last computer
That my dad will buy for me!

Our Computer Class

Our computer class met today
And I have to admit
That when the class was over
I didn't want to quit!
I love the feel of the keys
As I surf the web online.
It is so exciting
The information I can find!

Poems for the Classroom

Last Night

Last night I went to bed
With a poem in my head
I said "Oh, no." with a frown
"I'm just too tired to write this down!"

I tucked in my feet
And turned out the light.
And went to sleep
Feeling pretty bright.

I would awake
This thought I,
With a brand new verse
Just as easy as pie.

The words flew
Into my weary brain
And I had no doubt
I could remember them again.

Alas, this morning
I awoke with no clue-
What is a poor forgetful
Poet to do?

I don't remember a single verse
And to make it even worse,
I can't remember what the poem was about
So all I can do now is sit here and POUT!

Taste of Paste

I'm Giving Up Computers

I'm giving up computing-
It's making me quite sad.
I wrote a really long document
And was proud of what I had.
I tweaked it and I edited it
Until it looked absolutely precise.
I knew my teacher would like it
And think it was very nice.
But I hit the wrong button-
Oh, woe is me, alas, alack!
My whole document disappeared
To somewhere far away
And I cannot get it back!

Does Not Compute

This does not compute...
It seems like Greek to me
I don't know about bytes
Or what html might be!
I don't understand the language
Or how to install more RAM.
But wait! You can shop on this thing...
Hey! Here I am!!

**Computers are not intelligent.
They only think they are.**

Poems for the Classroom

My Hero

What Does A Hero Look Like?

What does a hero look like?
It's really hard to say.
A hero looks like the EMT.
Who goes to work each day.

A hero looks like a neighbor
Who is easily within your view.
A hero looks like a policeman
And a hero looks like YOU!

In Gratitude

Our thanks we give to our heroes
Who serve our country each day.
Our heartfelt appreciation we offer
For all they do and say.

Our appreciation is sincere
For we know that we should be
Offering prayers of gratitude
To those who help keep us free.

They do not all win medals
Or make the evening news at 10.
They serve their country every day
And you call them your friend.

Did I Say "Thank You?"

<u>Taste of Paste</u>

In Honor of YOU!

Welcome home soldier.
You are a hero in this town.
That's why there are lot of ribbons
Yellow ribbons scattered all around.

It matters not how you arrive here.
If you come by train or sea or air.
You will see them at each station. dock or depot
You will find them everywhere!

These ribbons helped to remind us.
While you were gone away.
That you were fighting for us
And that for your safety we should pray.

They reminded us of the families
That claimed you as daughter or son.
And that you were precious to them
Yes. each and every one!

They are bright like the sunlight
And float gently in the breeze
Held tight by doors and lamp posts
And by both fat or skinny trees!

Welcome home soldier.
You are a hero in our town.
People here will be shouting welcome back
Before your feet can touch our ground!

Hey, Hey You're My Hero!

148

Poems for the Classroom

Heroes

When we remember our nation's heroes
From that cruel September day.
Let us realize that men of valor
Do not instantly become that way.

A hero is not created in an instant
One deed and then it's done.
A hero's compassion is instilled at birth
His deed shows us that he's one.

There are heroes in training all about us.
In sizes large and small.
Some who are but infants now
Will someday answer a hero's call.

The ones who serve daily as fireman.
As policeman and EMT's.
As circumstance and duty calls them out.
Heroes they soon could be.

Consider the military men and women. too.
Who daily risk their lives for you.
Theirs is such a daunting task.
But never for accolades do they ask.

Look at your fellow passengers on a train
Or those who travel with you by air.
Look at the seats around you.
A hero may be sitting there.

A hero is built within the heart
And let us not forget.
They live with us and surround us...
We just don't know it yet!

Taste of Paste

Sports and Sportsmanship

The Coach

A coach is such a special person
With a character strong and unique
A voice that commands respect
And attention when he must speak.

He must have strength of character
And a mind that is able to discern
The abilities of his team
And what each member can learn.

He must be above reproach
An example to those he will lead
Able to see from observing
Just what each of his charges will need.

A coach is a valuable treasure
Worth his weight in pure gold
For he has the rare opportunity
Kids characters to meld and to mold.

**I love the way you look
As you play soccer
with the team.
I love to cheer for you
and then I love you
whether you lose or win!**

Poems for the Classroom

To A Wonderful Coach

How do you say thank you
To someone so grand
A leader, a mentor
A wonderful man!

How does one thank you
For all that you've done
To make life so special
For a brother or son?

We can't find the words
To say from our heart
But hope that this album
Will do it in part!

Cheers

You are always ready to cheer on our team
And to fill the day with fun.
You are each so special
Every single one!

Your talent is exceptional
Your spirit is contagious
Your enthusiasm is inspiring
And your moves sometimes outrageous!

We love our cheerleaders
You add so much to the fun
A game without your enthusiasm
Would be like summer with no sun!

Taste of Paste

A Coach

A coach must have sharp eyes
To see that which must be seen
And have a teaching spirit
To instruct in how it should have been.
A coach must have a listening ear
To hear the signs of stress or discontent
Ears tuned in to hear what was said
But sensitive enough to know what was meant.
A coach is eyes and ears and wisdom
But this is only one small part
For what makes a coach a winning coach
Is a loving, caring heart.

When Shawn is at Bat

When Shawn is at bat
The world stands still
If only for a minute
The stillness brings a special feeling
And Shawn revels in it.
Shawn doesn't hear the crowd
And to him no one else is there
His ears and eyes are tuned
Toward that ball coming through the air.
His family waits in anticipation
To see how he will do
As Shawn concentrates
On the task at hand
And hits a run or two.

Poems for the Classroom

Gymnast

A gymnast is a special girl
With strength of body and soul.
It takes a lot of inner strength
To retain her outer control.
Her mind is sharp and her body strong
Her focus never wavers
As she stands upon the floor
And every moment she savors.
Whether in a practice session
Or in a scheduled meet
Her spirit is always willing
And she's ready to compete.
We cheer her on each day
From the sidelines as we watch her
Our sport, our competitor and our hero
Our special gymnast daughter!

I Love the Way You Look

I love the lessons that you learn
As you play your game.
The soccer season for me
Will never be the same.

So go ahead my son and play
To your heart's content.
And I will be here to root for you
And consider the time well spent!

Taste of Paste

Basketball

You are such a special person
And you have such strength in you
To play this difficult game
With skill and grace as you do!
You are always focused on the goal
That is ahead of you
Your teammates depend on your skill
And you always come through.
You are always ready to compete
And do the best you can each day
Whether it is in practice
Or in a tournament you play.
You are worthy of our cheers
And we loudly send them your way
Our sport, competitor and our hero
We applaud you every day!

**Now that you
Have become
A soccer-playing son,
I have a new team
To cheer for
As I root
For your team
To be number one!**

Poems for the Classroom

Ski Patrol

The ski patrol is after me–
I see them bearing down.
It's probably because
I'm skiing upside down.

This isn't how I meant to ski
I really don't know how.
I ended up this way today,
But I can't change it now!

I started out the normal way
As I rode on the lift.
But once I tried to get off the thing
The wind began to shift.

So there I was and here I am–
Topsy turvey in every way.
I don't think I shall ski again
Once I get home today!

Sports

I love most kinds of sports
And some I do quite well
I find people in every single sport
Who have a great story to tell.

Be A Team Player!

Cheering You On (Sister)

You are my sister and my friend
And I watch in admiration-
The sportsperson that is you,
Keeping your strength and body in shape
For the sports you love to do.
I have been your cheerleader
As I've watched you through the years.
And I must admit as I see you graduate
I've shed a few sisterly tears.
Your skill in your beloved sports
Is quite impressive to see
But I'm more in awe as I look at you
Of the sister you are to me!

Cheering You On (Daughter)

You are my wonderful daughter
And I watch in admiration
The sportsperson that is you
Keeping your strength and body in shape
For the sports you love to do.
I have been your cheerleader
As I've watched you through the years
And I must admit as I see you graduate
I've shed a few motherly tears.
Your skill in your beloved sports
Is quite impressive to see
But I'm more in awe as I look at you
Of the wonderful daughter you are to me!

Poems for the Classroom

I Love to Cheer

Some people like ballroom dancing
And others like to sing.
Some prefer to tango
While others like to swing.

But I love to cheer.
I love the way it feels
To cheer for your team.
And dance and sing.
Oh, it's an amazing thing!

Cheer Coach

Look at the cheer coach
Knuckles turning white.
Grasping at the railing
As she watches her girls tonight!

She loves the excitement
But there always is the concern
That all safety precautions are in place
As their routines they learn.

She says a little prayer
At each and every routine.
Wanting safety for each girl
On her very special team.

Sing out loud and clear
Let us hear a roaring cheer!

Taste of Paste

Soccer kids

Look at them!
Aren't they great!
The way they play
Is truly first rate!
Two healthy kids
Loving the fun
Of playing soccer
In the sun!
I can hardly wait to see
What kind of players
They will be
As they mature and play
The games of life
From day to day!

Skateboarding

I wanted to go skateboarding.
But I kept on falling!
I think I'll probably give it up–
Don't seem to have the calling!

I'd Rather

The sun came up
And I crawled out of bed
Time to go to school
I'd rather play ball instead

Poems for the Classroom

A Little Boy's Prayer

Help me God to be today
A really good sport in every way.

I know that winning can be fun
And would love to once be Number One!

But deep inside this heart of mine
I only want what you design.

So as I kneel before you now
I ask you Lord to show me how–

How to run a race or play a game
Where win or lose. I feel the same.

Help me to cheer the others on
And keep me from jealousy so wrong.

Help me to cheer when they're ahead
And feel happiness for them instead.

So Lord please let my heart be able to enjoy
The trophy going to some other boy.

And please Father. let them see
That it really is all right with me.

For whether on the field or in the crowd
I want to make my parents proud!

Amen!

Taste of Paste

Time For Fun
Our Hike

Some people like to ride their bike
But as for me. I love to hike.
I went hiking with my best friend
For miles and miles before the end.

We looked at grass and trees and butterflies
And laughed and giggled. my friend and I.
As we counted the clouds up in the sky
And the time just seemed to fly!

I have no idea how far we went
But it was surely time well spent!
And I can't wait to hike again
Especially with my best friend!

Picnic in the Park

Oh what fun to picnic in the park!
Oh what a wonderful way
To enjoy the sun and have some fun
And spend a lovely day!

Oh what fun to sit in the grass
And drink lemonade in the shade!
What fun to eat from a picnic basket
Things so lovingly made!

But the most special thing
That ever I could do
Is to go on a picnic
In the park with You!

Poems for the Classroom

I Prefer the Slide

Some people say they love to swing
While others like to ride
The horses on the merry-go-round
And others love the slide.

When I go to the park.
The most fun I have found.
Is climbing to the slide's tip top
And then zooming to the ground.

So happily I slide along
And too quickly do I land
On my feet or on my bottom
In the nice warm sand!

I do not hesitate at all
To go back up again
But slides like every other game
Are more fun with a friend!

Playground Fun

Oh how I love to swing on the swing
And go up in the air so high!
I think that someday when I swing
My feet might touch the sky!

I love to slide down the slide
And land on the soft brown sand.
I like to go zooming down the slide
And I like it when I land!

I like to sit on the grass and play
And find a bug or two.
I love to go to the playground
'Cause there's so much for a kid to do!!

Taste of Paste

Dear Parents

We are going on a field trip.
We are going to the zoo.
We need this permission slip.
So that your child can go too.

We will be leaving bright and early.
So please be here on time.
For traffic could be difficult
And parking is hard to find.

We also need some mothers-
To come along with us.
To chaperone the kids at the park
And keep order on the bus.

Our Field Trip

Our field trip is over-
It really went well!
Boy, do I have
Wonderful stories to tell!

We saw all the animals
And caught lots of shows.
And the children watched quietly
All lined up in rows!

We chatted with parrots
And cockatiels.
And the children all know
How a baby chick feels!

continued...

Poems for the Classroom

...continued from previous page
They listened intently
To all of the spiels
And not one of the chaperones
Had to take headache pills!

All in all it went smoothly
And not one child had a fit
And we got them home safely
Not one did we forget!

What Could Be More Fun

What could be as much fun
As a day at the zoo?
Watching to see
What the monkeys will do?
What fun to watch
A giraffe so tall
Or to see a Panda
Curled up in a ball!
I love to see
Lions and tigers-Oh my!
And the snakes are so scary
But I didn't cry!
I loved the birds
High up in the trees
And the penguins so cold
That I thought they would freeze!
But my favorite thing
About the trip to the zoo
Was all of the fun I had
Being there with you!

Taste of Paste

Animal Soup

Speedy

Speedy is our hamster.
Our first pet is he.
He's a pretty nifty hamster.
I'm sure you will agree.

He has a wheel to run in
And in circles Speedy goes.
Until he gets tired of play
And crinkles up his nose!

We can't take him for walk
On a leash out in the park.
And unfortunately he likes to play
At nighttime when it's dark.

But we love Speedy
So very, very much.
He's a bit of furry love
That we can pet and touch!

Lullaby

I heard a frog singing in the night
Sister heard a cricket
When she turned out the light
Mommy sang to us
A night time lullaby song
And all of the outside creatures
Joined in and sang along!

Poems for the Classroom

I Hate Spiders

I hate spiders.
I hate the way they look.
Every time I see one.
I slap it with a book!

Teacher says they are God's creatures
And deserve to live and be free
Well. I don't mind their living
As long as they live far away from me!!

A Spider

A spider is a delicate masterpiece
It can spin a dainty web so wide
That is so beautiful. yet strong
To catch it's prey inside.

A spider is so misunderstood
By mankind here on earth
It's just doing the task
For which it was designed at birth.

Spiders

Boys love spiders
And snakes and such.
I can't stand a spider
And a snake I'll never touch!

Why can't boys love cuddly critters
Instead of bugs and snakes?
A boy starts out on a search for critters
As soon as he awakes!

Taste of Paste

Seals

What do seals eat?
They eat fish
But not on a platter
Or a pretty little dish!
They eat fish
Not cooked at all
I couldn't be a seal
And eat fish that's raw!

Good Fins

Look at me swimming with the fishes-
I'm glad they don't like dishes
Of little kids for dinner every day.
For that would surely keep me away!

I'm in the water like an otter
But I'm really mommy's daughter
Who just likes to splish and splash
In the water every day!

So won't you come and join us
Not a single fish will fuss.
If you make a splash when jumping in.
Then we can all be good "fins."

To swim like a fish Or to fly like a bird Is every kid's wish!

Poems for the Classroom

Swimming With the Dolphins

If from cares you want to get away
Come out with the dolphins and play!
They don't mind it at all if you stay
And see how they spend their day!

They are so wonderfully unique
And soon you will love "dolphin speak"
As they play with each other
You'll feel like a big brother
It's an experience that can't be beat!

If you want a dolphin kiss
I think I would be remiss
Not to tell you to rethink your wish
For their breath smells strongly of...
FISH!

Bugs

Moms don't always understand
Why a bug seems to be in demand
To a boy who loves to run and play
And gather little bugs throughout the day.
To Mom a bug is yukky stuff
And she just isn't tough enough
To hold or cradle a bug in hand
Like her bug loving little man.
For be it a firefly, beetle or ladybug
I've found you just can't hug—a bug!

Taste of Paste

Glad I'm Not A Bug!

Every time I get a hug,
I'm so glad I'm not a bug!

A bug can be quite cute I know,
But no emotions do they show.

A bug is usually much too small,
To do anything but slowly crawl.

I like to pick them up and check them out.
To see what a bug is all about.

But even though they may be snug,
I'd rather be me than the very best bug!

Glad I'm Not a Boy

I'm just a little bug
Content as a little bug can be.
To live my life
Free from strife-
Happy and carefree!

I would find no joy
In being a boy.
And having to go to school.
Spending the day
All locked away
Obeying rule after rule!

Poems for the Classroom

Scouting

Girl Scouts

She looks like such a little girl.
But the smile on her cute face.
Says that in scouting
She has found something to embrace.
She meets with her friends
And they have a lot of fun.
While at each meeting.
They have learned a lot
Before the meeting was done.

She is proud of her uniform
And thinks her pins are delightful
She loves having her own handbook
And finds it quite insightful.
She looks forward to the day
When a Junior Girl Scout she will be
And tries her best at her tasks to excel
And enjoy each Brownie opportunity!

It's Not All Cookies!

People stand in line for cookies
And we have the very best.
So beautifully presented
And easy to digest!

But scouting goes on all year long
And helps us each to grow
It's not all about the cookies—
Just thought that you should know.

Taste of Paste

The Best Season

Winter, Summer, Spring and Fall.
But the best season
of them all,
In my opinion has to be
The season of
The GIRL SCOUT COOKIE!

Scouting Helps Me

Being a girl scout is fun
And we enjoy being together.
But we work to earn our badges
On everything including the weather.

There is so much we need to learn
To help us every day,
And scouting gives us a boost
In a very wonderful way!

Congratulations to Our Girls

Congratulations to each of you
Who have been so busy this year,
Moving upward together
In your scouting career.
We are all so proud of you,
And your talent we want to proclaim
As we see 'cadette' after your name!

Poems for the Classroom

Proud As Can Be

You are ready now for a new adventure
And a new era in your life has begun.
Move forward in your usual confident way.
And enjoy the challenge and the fun.

You have strength and character.
And your spirit is gentle and sweet.
This is a winning combination
And you are wonderfully unique.

Stand firm always in your convictions.
And continue to be true to who you are.
Know that your parents stand beside you.
And in life you will go far.

We are so proud of who you are
And who you will yet be.
We congratulate you on your graduation-
The best is yet to come. you'll see!

Congratulations

Congratulations! You did it!
You are on your way!
Life is your oyster
And you are the pearl today!
We are so very proud of you
And we know you will go far
Know that we love you so very much
The lovely person that you are!

Taste of Paste

Boy Scouts

Scouts are awesome boys
Who strive to live each day.
No matter what the situation
In the most honorable way.

They are to be commended
On the way they choose to be.
And they serve as fine examples
For the youth of the community.

So if you see an eagle.
Flying high as eagles do.
Think about the Eagle Scout
And the example he sets for you.

Cub Scout

Congratulations Cub!
You are on your way!
We know you will be
An Eagle Scout some day!

Keep on track
And keep on trying.
And you will make it
There is no denying!

Congratulations Cub—
You are on your way!

Poems for the Classroom

We Are So Proud!

Just a little verse to say
How proud we are of you today!
You worked so diligently and did your best
On every task and every test.
You have studied so very hard
And countless others have inspired.
You set out to reach your goal
And stuck to your purpose with great control.
We support you in everything you set out to do
And all of this applause is just for you!

Getting Started

Every worthy task you start
Is first planted in your heart
Getting started in scouting.

Getting started and keeping on track
Is key to your success.
Be active in your troop, team, crew, or ship
Doing the things you do the best!

Live by principles of the Scout Oath
And use them in your daily life.
Be known as a peacemaker
Who never causes strife!

Work for those merit badges
And embrace responsibility
And an Eagle Scout
Soon you will be!!

Taste of Paste

One Great Step

This is just one of many
Wonderful accolades you will receive
For you are such a wonderful young man
And in your success we believe.

It is with great pride
That we celebrate with you today
Your receiving of the great honor
That is to come your way.

We are so pleased with your dedication
And thrilled with your integrity.
And every time we hear the term Boy Scout
We know that it fits you to a "T."

Congratulations as you move up
And as you receive your Eagle badge tonight.
Know that our prayer for you
Is that your goal always
Would be to do that which is right.

The First Step

The first step toward a goal
Is the most important one.
For you must get started
Before your task is done.
The first step you take to that goal
May seem so small to you.
But it is one step closer to the task
And you must see it through.

Poems for the Classroom

'Smore Verses

No campout would be complete
Without this yummy tasty treat!
No matter if you eat one or four
I guarantee you'll want 'smore!

Of the things one remembers
About when they were just a kid
Things that bring back pleasant memories
Of fun things they did.

So many happy memories
Were formed around a fire
Making little campfire treats
Until they began to tire.

Singing campfire songs at night
Until their throats were sore
And then stuffing their tummy full
With 'smore and 'smore and 'smore!!

I love the smell of a campfire
In the great outdoors
I love the fire, the glow of the flames
But most of all, the 'smores!
They taste so very yummy
And they look so totally neat
That they deserve some recognition
For being the world's hottest treat!

Taste of Paste

Miscellaneous Poems
Paper Sniffer

I love the smell of paper
It's music to my nose.
I sniff it at the store
And say, "I'll take one of those!"

Some papers have a musty smell.
While others smell like glue.
Some papers have just one aroma
While in others there are two.

Some papers smell like flowers.
With a fragrance that is sweet.
While some smell like candy canes-
A pepperminty treat.

If you've never noticed
Let me give you this advice-
Become a paper sniffer
Because paper smells really nice!

I have one question
To ask of you-
When you see paper
What do you do?

Do you hold it
And study the design.
Or is your nose for paper
As sensitive as mine?

Poems for the Classroom

Letting Go

I remember years ago
Your hand clutching mine.
As you first learned to walk
In the warm sunshine.
You teetered along.
With bits of success.
Your confidence grew
And you needed me less.
Then you were ready
To try it solo
How my heart ached within
Because I had to let go.
Years have passed since then.
It's your first day of school.
Excitement filled your eyes.
While I tried to play it cool.
It was a sunny Autumn day
As we walked through the doors.
My heart beat so quickly, and
My hand clutched yours.
The time came to quickly
To say our goodbye.
I still held your hand
And I refused to cry.
"I love you." I whispered.
You answered, "I know."
And my heart nearly burst.
Because I had to let go.

Anna Olson, by persmission

Jumping For Joy

The closest thing to flying,
My friend and I have found,
Is being totally in the air
With both feet off the ground!
It's the feel of being airborne
And even more fun when you land,
To know that your best bud has shared it,
For you did it hand in hand!

First Time Ice Skating

It looks so easy from the sidelines
As people waltz and glide around,
No one can tell you until you try it
Just how easy it is to fall down!

Gliding, flowing, smooth as silk,
I see it in my mind
And just about the time I glide,
I fall for the umpteenth time.

Then finally I'm moving smoothly
Gliding firm and strong,
And I grasp my sister's hand
And gracefully we move along!

I think I like this skating!
I think that I can do it well,
It may not be so difficult at all
But only time will tell!

Poems for the Classroom

Kid Stuff

I love to find a picket fence
With a gate on which to swing.
It doesn't matter if it needs some paint.
I find it's just the thing!

It gives my heart a happy song
To sing throughout the day.
As I lay atop the gate
And swing my cares away.

Siblings

Sometimes we don't see eye to eye
And don't hug cheek to cheek:
Words that sound a wee bit cross
Sometimes the two of us may speak.

We may have a spat sometimes
Or disagreements now and then.
And sometimes one might pout awhile
To see the other win.

But when nip comes down to tuck
The rest of the world doesn't mean the same
As we do to each other.
Cause no one is as special as
A sister or a brother.

Sibling Rivalry—Who Us?

Taste of Paste

Oh, My Tummy

It couldn't be the ice-cream
Or the soda pop
Or those little candy things
That looked like a lot of dots.
It surely wasn't the hot dog
Or the yummy apple pie
Perhaps it was the burger
And the extra big French fry.
But something that I ate today
Didn't settle right
But after I eat my dinner
I'll probably feel alright.

School Lunches

School lunches are yummy
I like them a lot.
They are quite tasty
And oft times they are hot!
I love eating in the cafeteria
With good friends each day.
My friends think that it's strange
That I feel this way...

UFO...
Unidentified Fried Object
Otherwise known as Lunch!

180

Poems for the Classroom

When I Grow Up

Construction Worker

I plan to be a construction worker
And build skyscrapers so very high.
That people in the buildings
Can see the planes go passing by!

I will search throughout the country
For special things to use
To create a special type of place
That folks will want to choose!

I will build in downtown areas
And on sunny shores as well.
I'll build malls for folks to shop in
Or homes where they will dwell.

I can see in my imagination
The things that I will do.
Perhaps someday I'll build
A home that is for you!

When I Grow Up

When I grow up
So big and tall
I want to play
Pro basketball!
I want to be a superstar
And travel with my team
Yes, that is it for sure—
To play basketball is my dream!

Taste of Paste

I Want To Be A Teacher

I want to be a teacher
When I'm as big as you.
And do all the wonderful things
That teachers get to do!

I want to ring a bell
And tell kids to come inside.
I want to watch at recess
As they play chase or hide.

I want to tell them about the world
And know all the important facts.
And have lots of books to read-
In fact I will have stacks!

I want them to remember me
As someone good and true.
In fact I want to be a teacher.
Because I want to be like you!

A Teacher

I want to be a teacher
And teach lots of kids each day.
I want to watch them as they work
And teach them games to play.
I want to teach in a school like mine.
And have lots of kids in class
Where I shall teach them all so well
That every one will pass!

Poems for the Classroom

Policeman

A policeman is what I want to be.
To keep our cities safe and free.
To keep cars from running traffic lights.
And keep our citizens safe at night!

I want to drive in a big ole car
With a siren that goes on top.
And I want people to pull over
If I tell them they should stop!

But most of all I want to be
A policeman who is friend to all.
And wear my city's uniform
Standing proud and tall!

I Want To Be

I want to be in movies
I want to be in a show
I want to work side by side
With famous people that I know.

I want my star on Broadway
And my name up in lights
I want to be a star
In which the world delights!

When I Grow Up
I Want To Be Just Like You!

Taste of Paste

I Want To Be A Nurse

I want to be a nurse
And help people
Who are ill.
If they need someone
To help them
Then I will.
I want to teach them
About good things to do
For a healthy body and mind
And I shall encourage them
Good exercise to find.

When I Grow Up

The world is full of possibilities-
So many things to choose from
As to what I'd like to be-
And I am also—a possibility!
Shanda wants to be a pilot
And fly across the land
Jon wants to be a rancher
And own a lot of land!
Jamie wants to be a fireman
And so does Wendy Sue
Cathy wants to join the Navy
And sail the ocean blue.
As for me. I really like
To write short stories and rhymes
So perhaps being a writer
Is how I shall spend my time!

Poems for the Classroom

Off to College

Be kind to this college student
As she leaves for school today!
I enjoyed having her close to home
And near us every day!
I know that it may seem silly
To mourn the passing of the years
And to miss someone as they go off to school...
And to shed these motherly tears.
After all. we raised her for this day
Prepared her from infancy on
To be self-sufficient. confident
Reliable and strong!
But I was not prepared
To see her drive away.
I was not prepared at all
For this milestone day!
Her empty room is hard to face
As is the empty chair
The bathroom's always free now...
No teenager drying her hair!
I cried as I watched her drive away
Those tears I still feel on my face.
Each time I find comfort in remembering
The warmth and strength of her embrace!
God bless my grown up child
I give them Lord to You
And ask that you watch over them
As only You can do.
And heal this mother's heart Dear Lord
That hurts so very much
And when I get too anxious Lord
Please let me feel Your touch!

185

Taste of Paste

Difficult Situations

Chosen Last

When he came home from school
His mother knew it right away.
Something had gone wrong
While he was at school that day.
She waited until at last
Her child would choose to speak.
And as he spoke big salty tears
Splashed down his trembling cheek.
She leaned close with listening ear
Waiting with loving heart to hear.
And when the tears were finally past
She heard him whisper
"I was chosen last."
Oh. how sharp the pain she felt
T'was if it had just been yesterday
That she. too. had cried while saying those words.
"I was chosen last to play..."
God bless the child
God bless the child
Who's chosen last
Who can't hit the ball as hard
Or can't run as fast!
God bless the child who stands and waits
And looks longingly at closing gates
That welcome other kids in first
Oh. bless their hearts and heal their hurts!

continued...

Poems for the Classroom

...continued from previous page

Lord bless the child
Who feels sadness and shame
That no one wants
To call their name
Lord bless the child who's chosen last
And let those disappointments be in the past
And let each child, no matter what their previous hurts
Know the joy of being chosen first!

God Doesn't Choose Us Last

All of you that suffered so,
In present times or past,
Do not despair
For God was there
And He never chooses last!
Before the land and sea God made
And before the earth was done,
God knew just who we would be,
He knew us every one!
Every seed God plants on earth
And every baby girl or boy,
He knew about before the world was made
And His creation caused Him joy!
Men on earth may choose you last,
May cause you hurt and tears,
But you were created by the hand of God
And He holds you, oh so dear,
And not a single child of God,
No matter what man may say,
Was least in the sight of God above
Or last chosen in any way!

Taste of Paste

Birthdays

Something Special-Teen boy

There is something special
About reaching the teenage years
Something that we look forward to-
It speaks of changing gears.

No longer a pre-teen boy
And not a kid anymore.
These years are very special
With what they hold in store.

There is so much fun
To look forward to.
And we are excited
That it is happening to you!

Birthday Boy

Look at you!
You are all grown up!
You're twelve years old today
And I sit in amazement
That the time seems to have run away!

I do not want to hold you back.
I know that you must grow.
But be you 2 or 20
Just know I love you so!

Poems for the Classroom

Happy Birthday Teacher

Words just don't seem to be
Adequate to say
How wonderful you are
In every single way!

Words fail me when I try
To say that I am proud...
I hear them in my heart
But they seem inadequate out loud.

I've watched you through the years
When times were really tough
And when others might have quit
And said enough is enough.

But you carried on and followed through
And you make such a difference every day.
In all the young and special lives
That our Father sends your way.

I pray that on your birthday
And each day your whole life through.
That blessing upon blessing
God will bestow on you!!

Happy Birthday
Teacher Dear
May You Have A
Happy Year!

Taste of Paste

Birthday for Teacher

I tried to make a card for you
But words just didn't come.
It had to be just perfect
For such a special one!
I searched up and down
And high and low
To find a card for you.
I had in my mind just want I wanted
And nothing else would do!
But as luck would have it
My search was in vain
And now I have no card
And must try again.
So I am trying to tell you
You deserve a card that is the best.
For in the world of teachers
I'd choose you over all the rest!
May this birthday be special
And filled with joy and happiness.
For I'm really proud to say
My teacher is the very best!

The teacher I need
To succeed
Will be one
Who wants my success
As much as I do!

Poems for the Classroom

Happy Sixteenth Birthday!

What a wonderful time of life
Sweet Sixteen can be.
Full of fun and friends
And days that are carefree!
I'm proud to be a friend
To a wonderful girl like you.
And want for you the very best
Today and your whole life through!

Super Sixteen!

I've watched you reach this milestone
For my students are special to me.
And as your teacher
It has been a joy to see.
You have developed such confidence
And you are so self-assured.
I have watched as you progressed
And as you have matured.
You have been such a joyous addition
To my class and I'm delighted.
To share in birthday wishes
And for your future I'm excited!

Our Family

Our family through the years
Has had its share of laughter and of tears
But whatever we do and whatever the weather
We will come through the storms of life together.

Taste of Paste

A Gift for Teacher

I made you some Note Cards
As a Christmas gift.
I hope they will cheer you
And give your heart a lift.
Use them to write your Thank You's.
Don't just put them on a shelf
And there's no need to send me one-
I kept one for myself!

A Gift

A teacher gives a gift so rare
For it's her very life she will share.
Spending hours of time each day
Listening to what others say.
She spends hours in the classroom
Teaching our daughters and sons,
Trying to instill in them
Values appropriate for our little ones.
After she leaves the classroom
There is still so much to be done.
She is like a school mother
Remembering the needs of each one.
She tries to teach by example
As well as teaching the facts from books.
As each day in the classroom
Into eager faces she looks.
Teacher, what can I do for you
To help you understand
That I appreciate all you do
And I think you are grand!

Poems for the Classroom

Holidaze

Irish Poem

Shamrocks and stickers
Green hats and such.
Are just little doodads
That people can touch.
They don't make you Irish
But they do make you smile
After you wear them
For a little while!

Dress-Up Fun

What fun to dress up
And be something new.
What fun to be someone
Who's not really you!
What fun to be a tiger
And growl at the world
Or to be a princess
Instead of a regular girl!
What fun to go around
In the neighborhood and show,
My funny costumes
To the people I know!

Trick or Treat Day

I got a bag of candy for kids who came to my door
There was a bag full yesterday, but not any more!

St. Patrick's Day

'Tis a blessing to be Irish
No matter where you live.
For the Irish folks are loving
And the Irish love to give!
So if you see an Irish lad
Or lassie on this day
Give them a kiss upon the cheek
And your smile will last all day!

Lucky to be Irish

I'm so lucky to be Irish.
I think it's just the best
To have been born part Irish
And consider that I'm blessed!

The Blarney Stone

My daddy kissed the Blarney Stone
And passed his gift on to me.
He said that to be part Irish
Was to be my legacy.
Well. Daddy was so right
I am so lucky everyday.
That folks just take it as "blarney"
Most of the things I say!!
What would I need to have
To consider that I'm a lucky girl?
I don't need a lot of stuff...
But I guess if one is born part Irish
Then that is luck enough!

Poems for the Classroom

Thanksgiving

We cook a festive dinner
And set a fancy table.
Folks come from near and far.
As many as are able.
Good food and pleasant chatter
Help us to celebrate Thanksgiving.
But they are just a part-
The real Thanksgiving for us all.
Can only be found within our heart.

Turkey Tragedy

It started out like an ordinary day
With kinfolks coming to visit and play.
But before the dinner was on the table.
To divert an incident. I was not able.
The platter was piled high with turkey and dressing
And hubby was offering the Thanksgiving blessing.
When a terrible accident I could not avert
And we had to skip dinner and go right to desert!
I tripped on the dog
And out flew our dinner
So now after this holiday
We will all be much thinner.
I caused a world catastrophe
Of which I hate to speak.
It was the downfall of Turkey.
The breaking up of China
And the overflow of Grease!'

Taste of Paste

Thanksgiving At Last

Thanksgiving Day has come at last!
I've waited all year through.
To have this special holiday
To spend with each of you.
The dinner doesn't really matter
Although the turkey looks delicious.
And the other things on the table
Are beautiful and I'm sure, nutritious.
Family and friends are gathered-
My favorite people all in one place
Close enough to hug each one
And see the smile on each one's face.
That's what makes the day so wonderful
Although I love each special part.
The thing I love the very best of all
Is the happy feeling in my heart!

Christmas

Christmas time is special
And all the world seems blessed
With love and kindness
And seems at it's gentlest.
We seem more aware of others
And the needs that they have, too.
And our hearts search for kindnesses
And loving things to do.
But as we worship together
Let us resolve to do our part.
To celebrate Christmas all year long
By keeping it in our hearts!

Poems for the Classroom

Our Gifts

Washing the car.
Feeding the kitty.
Helping to clean.
Making things pretty.

Helping Mom in the kitchen
Or Dad in the yard.
Doing things for others
Isn't really hard.

Welcoming new neighbors.
Babysitting my brother.
Obeying God's Word.
And loving one another.

For Christmas this year
Will be only the start.
Of the holiday spirit
I plan to keep in my heart.

Let's all celebrate
With each loving act we do.
But keep on celebrating
The whole year through.

Holidays

We love holidays
'Cause school is out
And that's what they
Are all about!

Taste of Paste

Dear Santa Claus,

Please come to visit.
Don't forget me please!
We don't have a chimney.
So Mom sent you our keys!
After you put the presents
Underneath the Christmas tree.
Just pull the door closed behind you
And on the table please leave our key.

Dear Santa

Hanging on our door
Is a very special key
Mom says that it is magic
And only you can see!
Please use that key
When you come to visit me.
For we are a modern family
With no fireplace or chimney!

Dear Kids

Please don't worry about ole Santa.
If you don't have a chimney for me.
I can use your front door to visit you
For I have a magic key!

My Notes to Santa!

Poems for the Classroom

A Christmas Remembrance

Christmas time is a special time
That makes us pause and consider
The loved ones we hold dear.
Some may live far away
While others may be near.

So know that I am thinking of you
And I hold you in my heart.
On Christmas Day and every day
Though we may be far apart.

As you celebrate the season,
Pause a moment to remember me.
And hang a special little remembrance
On your Christmas tree.

Merry Christmas Mom
Merry Christmas Dad
You are the best parents
That a kid ever had!

I wish a very Merry Christmas
And a wonderful new year
With joy, peace and happiness
For you and all those

Taste of Paste

Merry Christmas

Mommy and Daddy,
Today at school I worked so hard
To create for you this pretty card.
I cut and pasted and folded just right
So that I could give it to you tonight.

I printed as neatly
As I knew how
So that it would show,
Just how much I love you
'Cause I wanted you to know!

Merry Christmas, Mom

Even though I'm much too old
To create a card at school
I thought I would do it just this once
Although I wouldn't as a rule!

I don't want the guys to laugh at me
And think I'm doing girly stuff.
But though I tell you how much I care—
I'm sure I don't say enough.

So, I'm pretending I'm making this card
To give to the cute girl two seats down
Whose company is greatly in demand
And that's why the front doesn't say to mom
I hope you understand.
Love... your little sugarplum

Hugs

The Perfect Gift

Everyone needs a hug
And it is the perfect gift.
It closes the distance
Between two hearts
And gives the soul a lift!

A Hug

Sometimes it seems
That nothing else will do.
Except to get a great big hug
And to give one, too!
So I'm sending you this hug.
Wrapped in love galore.
And will be watching to see
If you should be in need of more.

Just a Note

Just a little note to say
You really brighten up my day!
Your smile is always great to see
Especially when you smile at me!
Your laugh is like joy unfurled
Sharing your love with all the world!
You are such a wonderful and special friend
That in this card my love I send!

Taste of Paste

Everyone Needs a Hug

Sometimes I look around
And such together folks I see.
Nope. they couldn't possibly
Be a nervous wreck like me...
That business woman in her suit
Wearing those designer heels
Couldn't possibly feel the frustration
Of creating fast and frugal meals...
That mom pushing twins in a stroller
Looks so happy and content
If I told her work was stressing me out
Would she understand just what I meant?
The bus driver is so nice and funny
As he welcomes the riders on
And jokes as he takes their money
No way he would sing a sad song...
But perhaps the business lady
Has a boss that was discontent
With the way her work had gone
And her tears had just been spent...
And the meals still have to be prepared
For kids and spouse alike
Although they need not be frugal
There will have to be something quick tonight.
And perhaps the mom is balancing a budget
That is really hard to do
And the older kids are crying
To go to Disneyland or the zoo...
And maybe the bus driver has had his hours cut back.
But he doesn't want to pass his sadness on.
Yes. his day has its problems
And he would understand your song.
So as you look around you
Let your eyes on each heart fall.
And say a little prayer
That the Good Lord would hug them all!

Poems for the Classroom

Hugs For You

If you had a bad day
And you are feeling blue.
This big ole hug
Is especially for you!

If your parents don't understand you
Or your kids are being a pain.
If you are in the line of a storm
And feeling weary of the rain...

Or if you are just feeling a little nostalgic
And need to hear a kind word or two.
Then let this verse surround you
And give a hug to you!

Attitudes

Eternal Optimist

My friends say that I'm an optimist
And they know that I'm no phony.
If I find a yard of fertilizer.
I always look for the pony!

Find the good in all you can
And never be a quitter.
If you find a problem.
Find a way to make things better!

Taste of Paste

The Optimist

In a world that sometimes seems
To embrace cynicism above all.
It is hard to always be the optimist on call.
An optimist tries to see things in a positive light.
And believe that things will work out for the right.

We are sometimes called Pollyanna and told
In voices both loud and bold.
To take off the rose-colored spectacles of idealism
And get in touch with the world of realism.

But as optimists we look for the positive things.
As happiness to our world we strive to bring.
We need not give in to gloom or pessimism
When our heart is full of faith. love and optimism.

First Word

Don't let it be important to you
To get the last word in an argument
but rather try to be there with
The "first word" to encourage.
to cheer. to strengthen and to heal
when someone needs you!

Pleasant words are a honeycomb. sweet to the soul...

Proverbs 16:24

Poems for the Classroom

Fun to Read Aloud

The Downside of Being a Kid

Teachers have it made-
They are bigger than me by far.
They don't have to walk to school
For they can drive a car.
They don't have to stay after school
If they get into a jam.
And they don't have to fret
about their grades
The awful way I am!
Teachers get to eat their lunch
With teachers in the lounge
That is safely across the hall.
Safely out of the range of
Some kid's gross spitball!
Oh. I wish I were a teacher.
I think it would be so cool
And then. I wouldn't have to be
Just another kid at school!

My Little Brother Bit Me

My little brother bit me
He chomped down on my nose
When I offered him his bottle
And it hurt down to my toes!
I offered him a cookie
But he bit my thumb instead
I think I'll bandage up my face
And put the kid to bed!

Taste of Paste

Once I Met a Dinosaur

Once I met a dinosaur
As strange as it may seem.
I knew what he was immediately.
But he knew no human being.

He asked me to go for a ride
And I'm so glad I did!
For riding on a dinosaur
Is a cool thing for a kid.

We went up streets and alleyways
Causing quite a stir
Although the ride was bumpy
Since dinosaurs have no soft fur.

But soon it was time to go
And I had to send him away
Because I live in an apartment
And there was no place for him to stay.

Dinosaur Class

We studied about dinosaurs.
We learned about each one.
But the thing they have in common
Gives studying quite a twist.
Since we are studying a creature
That we know doesn't exist!

Poems for the Classroom

My Dog Bit an Alligator

My doggie found an alligator
Hiding in our refrigerator
And before I could say a word
There was an awful sound I heard.
I heard a bark and then a snap.
A moan as if caught in a trap.
A hiss and growl and howl or two
And before I knew what to do-
I saw the gator run for the door
With the doggie chasing to bite once more.
But he was stopped by the sight of me
And a big ole bat that he could see-
Which I had grabbed
To hit that gator
And while I didn't need it then-
I might need it later!!

See you later Alligator
I haven't seen you
in quite a while
And even if I did
I might think you
to be a crocodile!

Taste of Paste

I'm Teacher's Pet

Look at me
I'm the teacher's pet
I don't want you
To ever forget!

It doesn't matter
What you think anyway
I know that it's true
So that's what I say.

I'm not really this confident
As a general rule
But I know I'm the pet
'Cause my mom home schools!

My Kids

Johnny looked on Randy's paper
When he didn't see me look
And hid his cheat sheet
Behind his big notebook.
Randy saw me looking
But didn't want me to know
That he saw Johnny peeking
And he won't tell me so.
Susan was almost in tears
When she saw we had a test
And I know at lunchtime
I will have all of them at my desk!

Poems for the Classroom

Problem Child

He entered the classroom
With a loud boyish shout,
As if to warn me
What he was about.

His face was sun-kissed
Tan and well freckled.
And he stared at me
With a look that heckled.

His clothes were wrinkled
And his shoes were dusty.
His smile was crooked
And his elbows were rusty.

But once I turned around quickly
And got a glimpse of his heart unprotected.
It eased all of the judgment
Which on him I'd projected.

He talked out in class
And he was distant for awhile.
But one day I laughed at his antics
And was rewarded with a smile.

At the end of each day.
It was his needs I took home with me.
For I had a longing for him
To be all he could be.

continued...

Taste of Paste

...continued

In spite of or because of
Our rocky start,
We each wormed our way
Into the other ones heart.

At the end of the year
When we said our goodbyes,
There were tears welling up
In each of our eyes.

And a few years later
Summoned for Jury duty to report,
I found myself a juror
In Judge Kevin's court!

Never Give Up

Never give up on a child,
Never give up or despair
Even though there may be times
When you feel like pulling your hair!
For you just never know
What wonderful mind
God may have placed in your care!

**Keep on trying
Day by day
When things get tough
Look up and pray!**

Poems for the Classroom

I Was a Problem Child

Ms. Jackie's class in fifth grade
Was my last hope.
I was discouraged and miserable–
At the end of my rope.
I mustered up my courage
Striding into class with
What I hoped would be
A look of more confidence and self assurance
Than ever had belonged to me.
Ms. Jackie didn't change her look one bit.
When I marched in that day.
I waited all the hour
For some chastising remark
That she might say.
But she seemed not to notice
My clothes all wrinkled and dusty
Or the fact that I was not freshly scrubbed
And perhaps a wee bit rusty.
I made a silly joke one day
And waited for a reprimand.
When instead Ms. Jackie laughed so hard.
It seemed difficult for her to stand.
That was that day I fell in love–
Oh. not the romantic kind.
But the kind of love that realizes
A meeting of a kindred mind.

continued...

Taste of Paste

...continued from previous page

I cried when I left her class.
It just did not seem fair-
To pass her room in years to come
And see another kid seated there.
And even though I didn't keep in touch
By phone or note or letter.
We had a special meeting
Which was even better.
I saw a look of purest joy
A look of pride such as from a mother
When Ms Jackie appeared in my court one day
And we recognized one another!
The jurors were being selected
And I glanced around the room.
When suddenly my eyes caught hers
As if with a camera's zoom.
There sat my Ms. Jackie.
The best teacher I ever had.
She who instilled in me the desire to learn
And use the intellect I had.
She looked past the outer me
And saw the inner me instead.
She taught me how to hope and dream
And this is where it led.
I looked at the defendant.
A young man of 22.
And in my heart I said to him
If only, son, she had been
your teacher, too.

Poems for the Classroom

If I Could Go to the Zoo

I wish I could go to the zoo
And see a great big bear.
I'd take along a sandwich-
One that I could share.
I'd walk right up to the cage
And look him in the eye.
And say, "I love you Mr. Bear,"
And he'd like me by and by.
I'd sit and chat with him
And sing him a song or two.
If I could have just one whole day,
To visit at the zoo!

If I could go to the zoo
I'd visit with the elephants
I think they look so very cool
In their big ole baggy pants!
I'd walk right up to their cage
And yell to them really loud
'Cause with those great big ears
They could hear me in the crowd!
I'd say "Hi, Mr. Elephant,"
I think you are so neat.
But I'd be careful where I walked,
Cause they have enormous feet!
Just another thing
I could do,
If I could spend the day
At the zoo!

continued...

213

Taste of Paste

...continued from previous page

Oh. if I could go to the zoo,
I'd visit the lions and more.
I'd sit on a log and talk to a hog
And see if a gorilla will snore!
I'd pet the animals at the petting zoo
And ride the train through the park
I'd have such fun all day in the sun
And wouldn't leave until dark!

The Principal's Office

I have to go to the office-
To the principal's office I must go...
This happens really often
And I thought you ought to know.
I dread going to the office
As I feel the teachers stare,
I can feel the goose bumps
On my arms, almost everywhere!
I hear the kids all talking
As I pass them in the hall,
And I see some big boys laughing
As they toss back and forth a ball.
I try not to worry about the office
Or let it get to me this way,
For since I am the principal
I have to go there every day!

Poems for the Classroom

I Got Sent to the Office Today

Mommy and Daddy
Are going to be sad.
They might be shocked
Or even be mad!

Though I'm usually pretty good
As a general rule.
Today I got into a bit of trouble
While I was at school.

I didn't have my homework
For it blew out of my hand
And right through our front door.
Where the next door neighbor's dog
Ran after as it as it soared

The dog jumped and grabbed it
And took off across the lawn
And before I could grab him
The little mutt was gone!

I tried to track him down
But the bus was stopped outside.
And my Mom had already told me
That I'd better not miss my ride.

As I rode the bus to school.
I saw that silly dog—
My Math assignment in his teeth
Sitting on a log.

continued...

215

Taste of Paste

...continued from previous page

But when the teacher asked for it
I found that I just could not say.
That a dog had grabbed my homework
And then had run away.

So I just looked down at the floor
And gave a little sigh.
And that's why, at the principal's office
Here sit I.

The Un-School Day

Yesterday I got up to go to school
And didn't really want to go.
I knew that there would be a test
On things I did not know.

I told my mom that I was ill.
Both my tummy and my head.
Hurt me so awful much
That I should really stay in bed.

Up to my brow she put her palm
And amazingly she said
That yes indeedy, I was right
I belonged there in my bed.

Time for the school bus came and went
And I was still safe at home
Thinking smugly to myself
That about the house I'd roam.

continued...

Poems for the Classroom

...continued from previous page

But in came my mom with breakfast
Carried gently on a tray.
She reminded me that sick as I was
I should remain in bed all day!

She said that a quiet and tidy room
Was more restful to the ill.
So she took my noisy toys out of the room
Making it so silent and so still.

She said she would come back to check
And make sure my pillows were all fluffed.
To make sure the room was nice and dark
So that I'd get rest enough.

Ohhhh, the day was long and sad.
The day was so dull and boring
That before the awful day ended at last
Even my faithful dog was snoring!

When nighttime came at last
I said, "Mom, I'm feeling so much better.
It's all over now
Whatever was the matter!"

She smiled that Mothers' knowing smile
And sweetly looked at me
And with her palm up to my brow
She nodded to agree.

continued...

Taste of Paste

...continued from previous page

Morning came and the sun was up,
My how the time seemed to fly.
As I prepared to go to school
There was no happier kid than I!

I was ready right on time to catch the bus
Without delay or hint of fuss.
I waved goodbye from my window seat
Oh, freedom from that room was sweet!

I entered into my classroom on time
Feeling good and looking fine.
But waiting for those sympathetic looks
As I carefully got out my books.

But not one person mentioned that I hadn't been there
And I thought to myself, "Well, that isn't fair!"
Here I had been sick abed
And not one sympathetic word was said.

Then as I settled down at my desk,
Thankful that at least I'd missed that test.
"Good Morning Class!" I heard the teacher say,
"I hope you enjoyed yesterday!"

"I know that it must have been such a sweet surprise
To have that snowfall greet your eyes.
Knowing that you got the whole day off to play
And not worry about coming back to school until today!

And since you all had an extra day of rest
Please get out your pencils—we're having a test!"

Poems for the Classroom

Thank You From Thena

Thank you for letting me share with you! I hope you found a bit of wisdom as well as humor in these little verses. I hope that whether you were looking for something to teachers, about teachers, for students, that you found it here.

No school is separate from the parents of the students; therefore, parents are included in this book as well. I have been in all of those different roles, as I imagine, have a good many of you. It is my hope that you can identify with the poems within these pages.

These poems were written with smiles and sometimes outright laughter and others of the more serious nature with a few tear drops. Each one came from within my heart.

Love,

Thena Smith

Taste of Paste

About the Author
Thena Smith

Thena was born in a tiny farming community in Western Kentucky where she remained until she married her college sweetheart in 1965. For the last 20 years she has lived in Coronado, California with her husband, Ron and her daughter, Melissa. Thena remembers writing her first poem at the age of 7 for a class Christmas project. Her mom sent it to the local newspaper and it was published. For many years, she wrote, but failed to save her writings. Finally, encouraged by a friend to save her work, she along with friends, presented a collage of poetry and music that was televised on a local cable station. She also co-wrote a children's musical that was presented locally. Thena has always been a scrapper. And, as the hobby began to catch on, she began to share verses with others. A local on the scrapbooking message boards. Thena has written hundreds of poems to share with her many friends.

More of Thena's writings can be found in her two best selling books, "Where's Thena? I need a poem about..." and "Whispers." Can't get enough?? Watch for more of Thena's works to come at www.BluegrassPublishing.com.

Note from Thena: What a surprise when Linda found my website and contacted me about using some of my poetry in her books. I was even more amazed to find out that she lived in Mayfield, Kentucky, a few miles from Lowes, Ky. where I was born and raised. Isn't it funny that I had to move to California to meet her and she moved from California to Kentucky and ultimately met me. Amazing what a small world exists when God has a plan. Since our first lovely chat via e-mail, we are enjoying a blossoming friendship.

Poems for the Classroom

Our Favorite Sites

- 💡 Be sure to visit the websites of all of our contributing writers. You can find a link to more of their sites on our website at: www.BluegrassPublishing.com.

- 💡 Our favorite place for fonts is www.LetteringDelights.com. Doug and his company have the greatest selection of fun, funky and fabulous fonts for all your scrapbooking and crafting needs and wants. Be sure to tell them we said, "Hello."

- 💡 For the best in rubberstamps and related products, be sure to visit Posh Impressions, the website of Dee and Warren Gruenig. They are wonderful people and have lots of info and products available. Their website is: www.PoshImpressions.com. We love them!

- 💡 This is one of our favorite sites. At Cottage Arts make your memories into lasting works of art with digital scrapbooking ideas and products. You will be inspired! www.CottageArts.net

- 💡 Need a website created? Visit Holly VanDyne our great webdesigner. She is a joy to work with and will do all she can to help you develop the site that fits your needs. www.ScrapbookInsights.com.

Our Best Sellers!

We have the Largest Collection of poems & quotes for scrapbookers and cardmakers ever created!

The Ultimate Guide to the Perfect Word

(Our biggest seller—over 200,000 copies sold!)
Linda LaTourelle

The Ultimate Guide to Celebrating Kids I

(birth through preschool–384 pages)
Linda LaTourelle

Introducing the first book in our new
"Perfect Words Worth Repeating" series...

LoveLines

(artistic quotes to be used time and again)
Linda LaTourelle

Where's Thena? I need a poem about...

(insightful & witty poems)
Thena Smith

Whispers

(passionate poetry & words of love)
Thena Smith

Be sure to watch for all of our books on Shop At Home Network!

More Surprises Coming Soon!

New Books

Now Available

The Ultimate Guide to Celebrating Kids II
(All New—Grade School Age—384 pages)
Linda LaTourelle

The Ultimate Guide to the Perfect Card (2nd. Ed.)
(Revised edition—now 384 pages)
Linda LaTourelle & CC Milam

Board Smartz
(learning tips and bulletin board quips)
Thena Smith

Taste of Paste
(poems for the classroom of all ages)
Thena Smith

What Can I Say?
(words with an artistic flair!)
WendiSue

Coming Attractions

Season's Greetings
Linda LaTourelle

C is for Christmas
(poetry for the season)
Thena Smith

The End?

No Way—We hope that
Taste of Paste
will inspire you
to create boards
that will educate
and delight
your students
for years to come.

My Favorite Poems

My Favorite Poems

For more inspiration visit our website:

BLUEGRASS PUBLISHING, INC.

ORDER FORM

NAME			DATE	
ADDRESS				
CITY/STATE				
CREDIT CARD #			EXP. DATE	
PHONE ( ) —				
E-MAIL				

QTY	TITLE	EACH	TOTAL
	The Ultimate Guide to the Perfect Word BY LINDA LATOURELLE · OUR BIGGEST SELLER	$19.95	
	The Ultimate Guide to the Perfect Card BY LINDA LATOURELLE · NEW/BIGGER-384 PG	$19.95	
	The Ultimate Guide to Celebrating Kids I BY LINDA LATOURELLE · BIRTH TO PRESCHOOL	$19.95	
	The Ultimate Guide to Celebrating Kids II BY LINDA LATOURELLE · NEW/GRADE SCHOOL	$19.95	
	LoveLines—Beautifully designed quotes BY LINDA LATOURELLE · NEW/COPY & USE	$12.95	
	Taste of Paste: Poems for the Classroom BY THENA SMITH	$14.95	
	Board Smartz: Bulletin Board Tips BY THENA SMITH	$14.95	
	Where's Thena? I need a poem about... BY THENA SMITH	$19.95	
	Whispers: Passionate Poetry BY THENA SMITH	$12.95	
	What Can I Say?: Words With Artistic Flair BY WENDISUE	$12.95	

SEND ORDER TO:

BLUEGRASS PUBLISHING, INC.

(270) 251-3600
PO BOX 634
MAYFIELD, KY 42066
FAX (270) 251-3603

WWW.BLUEGRASSPUBLISHING.COM

6% TAX KENTUCKY	
$2.95 Per Book	S/H Disc. Given on 3 or more
TOTAL AMOUNT	
$	

Thank You
For Your Order